Hiking the Bitterroots

Mort Arkava

(3rd Edition)

This volume is dedicated to the memory
of my sister Sandra "Sandy" Arkava Santer

I would like to thank Linda and Mike Tiernan for their generous
help with this manuscript. I would also like to thank the following
US Forest Service Wilderness Rangers for their assistance: Marty
Almquist; D. L. Ferris; and Bill Goslin. Thanks are also due to
retired forest ranger Ed Bloedel for his helpful suggestions.

Published by:
Mort Arkava
Corvallis, Montana

Printed in the United States of America

Library of Congress Control Number 2001119957

ISBN Number 0-9677518-2-9

Cover cartoon and maps by:
Nancy Arkava

Table of Contents

INTRODUCTION

This book describes hiking trails in the Bitterroot Mountains of Montana and Idaho. Each hike narrative is depicted on one of the maps included in the last thirteen pages. The best map for planning trips in this area is the <u>Selway Bitterroot Wilderness</u>. Copies may be obtained from the Bitterroot National Forest, 1801 North First Street, Hamilton, MT 59840 or from the US Forest Service's Northern Region Office in Missoula, MT, or at Bitterroot Forest District Ranger Stations.

If you are planning any significant off-trail hiking, it's a good idea to obtain the topographic maps published by the US Geological Survey (USGS). Specific USGS maps are identified at the end of each hike.

A word of caution is in order here. You cannot count on the maps to always provide accurate trail information. The Selway-Bitterroot Wilderness Map recommended above is the best all-around map available for this area. However, it includes several trails that no longer exist on the ground and it omits several that do exist. These discrepancies are noted in this book.

I have personally hiked all of the trails covered in this volume. I have tried to present an accurate and up-to-date account of conditions. However, trail conditions are subject to change from one season to the next. Avalanches, floods, windstorms, and wildfire are some of the natural forces that may have considerable impact on trails. If you find major differences in trails, I would like to hear from you.

When to Hike. A major consideration in planning a hike in the Bitterroots is the time of year. Snow depths, ice, and stream flow levels are extremely important factors to keep in mind. Some of the lower lakes in the Bitterroots may be ice free by late May.

However, other high altitude lakes may still be frozen over in mid to late June. Further, many trails are snow covered well into July. Unfortunately there is no easy way to predict which hikes will be open as there is considerable variation from year to year. However, I can offer some general guidelines for trip planning.

For those hikes which involve crossing the crest of the Bitterroots, you can assume that the trails will be snow covered until mid July. In addition, if the hike involves fording any major creeks, the water levels may not subside before early August. Here are a few examples. In an average year, if your hike involves crossing the Bitterroots from Tin Cup Creek, Boulder Creek, or Watchtower Creek, it is unlikely that the trails will be clear of snow before mid July. If you plan to hike from Bear Creek Pass or Twin Lakes, it is unlikely that the Lost Horse road to the trailhead will be open before mid July. In the fall it is not unusual to get snow in late September or early October.

To find out the current status of a trail or road, you may call the Recreational Information Office of the Bitterroot National Forest in Hamilton at (406) 363-7117.

I hope you enjoy hiking in the beautiful Bitterroot Mountains. To help insure that we all enjoy our outdoor experiences, I ask that you help take care of this special place. Although the Forest Service is responsible for administering these lands, the forests and the wild places belong to all of us. It's up to all of us to take care of these precious lands. If others make a mess, help to clean it up. The Forest Service wilderness rangers have been encouraging campers to leave no trace of their visit to the wilderness.

1. North Fork Fish Creek

This is an easy hike following the North Fork upstream for 7 miles. The trail climbs at a modest rate gaining 1,200 feet in 7 miles, and provides good access to the creek in several places. The trail is easy to follow and well shaded. The area near Greenwood Creek is a good place to camp, making this a good choice for novice backpackers. Refer to Map # 9.

Distance: 7.

Trailhead Directions. Take Highway 93 to Lolo, 10 miles south of Missoula. Turn onto Highway 12 and drive west 25 miles to the signed Fish Creek Road, located 1 mile past Lolo Hot Springs. Turn right on Fish Creek Rd. #343. At the top of a steep hill is a three- way junction. Take the middle fork, which is 343, and drive 22 miles north to the signed West Fish Creek Road. Drive 7 miles west, passing Hole in the Wall Lodge at 6 miles and continue past the cluster of cabins to reach the Forest Service campground. Park near the signed trailhead. There are stock facilities, campsites, a well and an outhouse, with plenty of room to park. There is also a Forest Service Guard Station just beyond the campground.

I-90 alternative access. Drive 38 miles west of Missoula on I-90, turn off at the Fish Creek exit. Drive south 10 miles to West Fish Creek Road. Turn right and follow the directions above.

Trail Description. The sign for trail #103 is located next to the entrance road. The path starts in heavy forest passing close to the fenced pasture in back of the ranger station. After one half mile the trail draws close to the North Fork. At one mile there is a signed junction for Strait Creek Trail. Stay right for Trail #103. The route follows a more uneven course after the junction, rising and falling in order to climb above the rock cliffs next to the creek. The North Fork is a very attractive stream, with a relatively wide flood plain for the next three miles. The trail is mostly shaded by large trees and lined with ferns.

At 3 miles the canyon narrows. The trail contours along the hillside above the stream. At 4.5 miles it drops down closer to creek level. At 6 miles you reach an attractive meadow with two log cabins next to the trail and the remains of a nearby outbuilding partially obscured by the trees. One of the cabins had a tarp on the roof, a good stovepipe, and glass in the windows. Both appear relatively weatherproof and are secured by locks. This is the Greenwood cabin area and these are the remains of earlier mining efforts.

At 6.2 miles you reach Greenwood Creek, a small shallow stream offering an easy but possibly wet crossing. The trail passes several small meadows which would make excellent campsites. The trail is shaded by a canopy of cedar trees. At 7 miles French Creek can be crossed on a convenient foot log. Just past French Creek there is an unsigned trail junction. This is the trail leading to French Lake located almost 3 miles west.

Map: USGS Straight Peak.

2. Cache Creek

This is a very pleasant, easy trail gaining little elevation for the first 3 miles, and only climbing about 700 feet over 5 ½ miles. The route traverses a heavily forested area and is pleasantly shaded in summer. The trail follows the creek closely enough for continued access. The wide flood plain and related willow flats are somewhat unusual for mountain streams in the Northern Rocky Mountains. The stream access appears to offer easy fishing opportunities. Old silver snags attest to the cataclysmic forest fires of 1910. This trail should hold great appeal to those who enjoy a combination of hiking and fishing. Refer to Map # 10.

Distance: 5.5.

Trailhead Directions. Take US 93 to Lolo located 10 miles south of Missoula. Turn west onto US 12 and drive 25 miles to the signed Fish Creek Road, just west of mile marker 7. Follow Fish Creek Road # 343 north. At the top of a steep hill is a three-way intersection. Take the middle fork which is 343. Drive 11 miles north and turn left on Montana Creek road # 4218. This road is signed for Cache Creek. Drive up the very steep hill 0.5 mile to the Y junction, take the unsigned left fork and follow the road 0.7 mile to the end of the road. The trailhead features a large parking area with room for at least a dozen cars. There is a stock ramp, a hitch rail and a trailhead sign, but no other facilities.

Trail Description. Follow the trail downhill from the parking lot along an old overgrown jeep road for the first half mile. The slope is very gradual and the path is nicely shaded by heavy forest. At 0.5 mile the trail crosses Montana Creek. There is a crossing log in a brushy area downstream from the stock crossing.

The trail continues to follow Cache Creek upstream with good access. Cache Creek is an attractive meandering trout stream with deep holes at each bend. The smooth trail offers easy and pleasant hiking along it's shaded path.

At 2 miles there is a small stream crossing. The flood plain for Cache Creek then expands into wide willow flats. In places the flood plain is almost 200 yards across, with numerous beaver ponds. At 3 miles the willow flats end. The trail then draws closer to the creek as the canyon narrows.

Beyond 3 miles the trail climbs a bit more noticeably. At 4 miles the route climbs a short steep segment to briefly emerge from the heavy forest. Here the route offers views of the ridges and peaks towering above the canyon. The trail continues to gain elevation at an easy rate. At 5 miles there is a small creek crossing and at 5.5 miles it reaches Irish Creek where a convenient foot log offers an easy dry crossing.

There is an outfitters camp at the junction of Irish Creek and Cache Creek. I recommend you turn around here because the trail leading up to Cache Saddle has not been cleared for many years.

Map: USGS, White Mountain.

3. Lee Creek Interpretive Trail

This is an easy and pleasant loop hike providing information about a variety of trees. If you are unsure about identifying Lodgepole Pine, Douglas Fir, and Ponderosa Pine, this is your chance to learn how to recognize them. A self-guided tour supplemented by a pamphlet introduces an interesting variety of forest information and issues, while providing an enjoyable jaunt through the woods.

Distance: 2.5

Trailhead Directions. Take US-93 to Lolo located 10 miles south of Missoula. Turn west onto US-12 and drive 26 miles to the Lee Creek Campground located just west of mile marker 6. Drive into the parking lot just past the entrance. This is the trailhead for the Lee Creek Interpretive Loop and also for the Wagon Mountain Trail. A toilet and picnic facilities are located near the parking lot.

Trail Description. Walk up the campground road 100 yards to the trail sign and the box with the informational pamphlets. The trail climbs at a gradual rate, winding through the lodgepole grove. There are several intersecting trails and old roads near the start. The tour consists of 20 informational stations, each numbered with a sign. The route meanders through a variety of landscapes, including an area that was logged in 1964.

The trail climbs some gentle switchbacks and continues through a grove of large trees. A granite outcropping overlooks the upper reaches of Lolo Pass. The route continues through widely spaced Ponderosa and Lodgepole and then climbs gently along the ridge to a signed trail junction with the Lee Creek Ridge Trail at 1.25 miles. Take the right fork which leads downhill through a few switchbacks to a small footbridge where it briefly joins an old abandoned logging spur, reaching the Lee Creek Road at the base of a big ugly clearcut hillside. Turn right and follow the road back down to the trailhead.

Map: Lee Creek Interpretive Trail Map, US Forest Service.

4. South Fork Lolo Creek to Bass Creek

Although a few portions of this hike are marred by evidence of dam construction or logging activity, much of the trail offers grand vistas and the pleasure of walking through pristine scenery. The trail has a number of attractive campsites, especially along the less-traveled South Fork-to-Bass Lake segment. This segment also provides a chance of viewing elk or moose. Some interior parts of this trail are not well maintained; the entire Bass Creek leg, though, may be followed easily. Use is heavy from Bass Lake to Bass Creek trailhead. From South Fork Lolo Creek to Bass Lake, use is very light.

Distances (from S. Fork Lolo Creek trailhead): See Map #1
Lantern Creek *3½*
South Fork Lolo Creek *4*
Unnamed lake north of Bass Lake *11*
Bass Lake *12*
Bass Creek trailhead *20*

Trailhead Directions. South Fork Lolo Creek end. From Lolo, drive 10.5 miles west on Highway 12 to Elk Meadows Road. Turn south (left) and drive 2.6 miles to South Fork Lolo Creek Road. Then turn left and drive 1.9 miles to the trailhead, which is marked with a Forest Service sign. There is ample parking, a horse ramp, and a camping area.

Bass Creek end. Drive from Florence on Highway 93 to the Bass Creek Road, four miles south. Turn west (right) and drive 2.5 miles to the trailhead at the west end of Bass Creek campground. All usual campground facilities are available here, including a horse ramp and plenty of parking space.

Trail Description. From the South Fork trailhead, the trail starts on an old jeep road and maintains a fairly even grade for the first one-quarter mile, then begins a very steep climb for the next two miles through a large clearcut area. After a steady climb, at two miles the clearcuts end and the trail intersects the Lantern Ridge trail, which leads east to the Mill Creek trail and then to the Lolo Peak trail. This junction is signed. Hikers going to Bass Lake should stay on the main trail, heading south.

The trail follows the west face of a ridge high above the south Fork of Lolo Creek, climbing gradually but steadily, mostly in trees, but allowing occasional glimpses of the high peaks to the south. Then

8

it wanders through a nice stretch of open hillside among widely spaced giant ponderosa pines. Most of the drainage can be seen from a rocky lookout. At about three miles the trail begins a gradual descent. At 3.5 miles it crosses Lantern Creek, then descends steadily to the creek bottom to follow the south fork of Lolo Creek. At four miles it crosses the creek. There is a good campsite next to the creek. Shortly past a Wilderness Boundary marker is a partially collapsed log cabin. This is an excellent campsite.

At about five miles the trail breaks out of the trees and crosses a large, open meadow, where the creek winds gently through sweeping curves and deep pools with ideal fishing conditions. There are several fine campsites here. Just above the meadow the trail crosses the creek. There are scattered logs to walk upon above the horse crossing; this could be a difficult ford at high water, however.

From here the trail degenerates. It is rough, overgrown with brush, and poorly defined. It winds through marshy places, then crosses the creek again at about seven miles. For the next two miles the course runs through large, open meadows that alternate with patches of heavy timber. The meadows appear to have been created by snow avalanches cascading down the steep canyon walls. This is ideal country for elk and moose. It is well watered even in the late summer, with tall grass in the meadows and excellent cover in the cool, shady forest.

At about eight miles the trail leading to Bass Lake is reached. There is a sign for Bass Lake here. The trail leaves the creek and heads uphill, following a blazed trail that switchbacks through the forest, climbing very steeply. (Note: Travelers who miss the trail here may be fooled into taking an old, poorly defined trail following the South Fork of Lolo Creek to its headwaters at the South Fork Lakes. This is a very rough trail, traversing wild country with heavy timber and brush cover. It is great for elk hunting but is difficult country for the casual hiker.) Watch for blazes and cairns marking the trail.

The climb to the top of the ridge above Bass Lake is fairly difficult. The distance from the creek bottom to the ridge crest is about three miles. Just before reaching the crest there is a small, unnamed alpine lake - a high, lonely spot. At its lower end is an excellent campsite. This spot is one of the most attractive campsites on this hike. A hiker planning to walk out through Bass Creek might consider camping here rather than at Bass Lake, which is less than a mile away but is very heavily used.

The trail goes around the small lake and over the pass to a ridge overlooking Bass Lake, then switchbacks down toward this large, deep lake. Halfway down, the hiker will reach a trail junction: the right fork leads around the upper end of Bass Lake. The left fork leads east toward the dam and then down Bass Creek to Bass Creek trailhead about seven miles east. The Bass Creek trail crosses the earth-filled dam to its south side, descends a steep hill for a few hundred yards, then crosses to the north side of Bass Creek again and descends gradually on a wide trail.

Throughout most of its length this trail follows an old road. This road was constructed with a bulldozer and provided access for the heavy equipment necessary to rebuild the earthen dam in the early 1950s and again in 1996.

The upper end of the Bass Creek trail presents a substantial esthetic contrast, where the dam squats in ugly juxtaposition to the splendor of the natural beauty: the huge, bare, earth-filled structure is surrounded by a raw, unattractive scar of cut trees and exposed gravel lacking protective grass or other growth. Yet countering this ugliness is the upper end of Bass Creek, a wide, beautiful mountain canyon featuring lovely open meadows and steep rock walls, and graced by a soft covering of trees and brush.

10

Topographic Maps. Camp Creek; Dick Creek; St. Joseph Peak; St. Mary Peak.

5. Mill Creek Lolo Area

There are two different Mill Creek trails covered in this book. This one is located in the Lolo Creek area between the South Fork of Lolo Creek and the Lolo Peak trailhead. The trailhead is located in a rural residential area and the parking is very limited. There are three trails available from this location. The first few miles of each of the hikes are through clearcuts and all three hikes involve lots of climbing. You may choose the trail to Lolo Peak or the trail to the junction of the South Fork of Lolo Creek. A third trail branches off the South Fork of Lolo Creek to the old Lantern Ridge lookout site. This is a very steep climb with picturesque views of mountain peaks. Use is light.

Distances: See Map #1
South Fork of Lolo Creek Trail Junction...........*8*
Lolo Peak Trail Junction *5*
Mormon Peak Trail Junction............................*6*
Lantern Ridge Trail Junction............................*4*
Lantern Ridge Lookout Site *6½*

Trailhead Directions. Drive 6.5 miles west on Highway 12 from Lolo. Turn south on Mill Creek Road. The road is signed. Follow this road through the rural residential area .6 mile to the locked gate. The sign here indicates this is the end of the county road. The old logging road behind the gate is signed as the beginning of trails 309 and 1310. There is no designated parking. However, because the road is a county right of way, you should be able to park on the roadside.

Trail Description. Follow the logging road past the walk through gate and through the clearcuts. At irregular intervals trail signs are posted on trees. About one-half mile past the gate a well defined path branches off to the left. This trail is a shortcut to eliminate several switchbacks on the logging road. Follow the trail south for another half mile. The trail cuts across the logging roads in several places and there are a few more trail signs. About one mile beyond the locked gate there is a sign for trails 309 and 1310. The trail junction is just beyond the sign.

To take trail 309, hike up the right fork. The trail crosses a good footbridge over Mill Creek just beyond the trail junction sign. About one-quarter mile past the bridge are the remains of a partially collapsed log cabin. Past the log cabin the trail begins to climb very steeply through two miles of clearcuts. At two miles the trail enters a forest of lodgepole pine and continues to climb.

About one mile past the end of the last clearcut, there is an old sign on a tree indicating the trail to the South Fork of Lolo Creek. Just past the sign is a trail junction. This side trail leads to the site for the Lantern Ridge lookout. There is no sign at this junction. This side trail climbs continuously and steeply for about three miles to a high, lovely site about one-half mile north of Lolo Peak. The trail ends at about 8,000 feet elevation in this alpine setting. Both Lolo Peak and its north ridge are very close by. There is no evidence of the Lantern Ridge lookout. The total elevation gain from the Mill Creek trailhead to this point is almost 3,900 feet in six miles.

To continue southwest on trail 309 towards the South Fork of Lolo Creek, hike past the lookout trail junction. The trail climbs at a more moderate pitch beyond the junction. About one-half mile past the junction the trail crosses a creek, and then another creek shortly beyond the first. About one mile past the trail junction is an old faded sign for the Lantern Ridge lookout. A dim trail follows the ridge towards the east. This trail joins the Lantern Ridge lookout trail mentioned above.

About 1.5 miles beyond the sign the trail starts to go downhill. The last mile before the junction is very steep with lots of switchbacks.

The South Fork of Lolo Creek trail junction is clearly signed. The junction is located at the upper end of a large clearcut. From here the trail goes down to the South Fork trailhead, two miles north. (For trailhead directions see South Fork of Lolo Creek). The hike back down to the Mill Creek trailhead is eight miles.

The left fork at the Mill Creek junction (trail 1310) leads to the junction with the Lolo Peak-Mormon Peak trail. The trail climbs steeply in places. The trail junction is about four miles southeast and the trail climbs about 2,300 feet. Parts of this trail are adjacent to privately owned land where extensive clearcut logging has taken place, however much of the route is in forest areas.

At the junction with the Lolo Peak Trail, you may elect to continue uphill towards Lolo Peak or to go downhill to the trailhead near Mormon Peak about three-quarters of a mile east. (For information about the Lolo Peak Trailhead access, see the Carlton Lake and Lolo Peak Trail description.)

Topographic   Maps.   Camp
Creek; Dick Creek.

6. Carlton Lake and Lolo Peak

The hike to Carlton Lake follows Carlton Ridge to its summit just below Lolo Peak. The views of the north ridge of Lolo Peak and

Lolo Peak itself are outstanding. Carlton Lake is located at the base of Lolo Peak and is used as a staging point for those climbing to Lolo Peak. Use is moderate.

Distances: See Map #1

Carlton Ridge..*4*
Carlton lake *5*
Lolo Peak *7*

Trailhead Directions. Drive to Lolo located south of Missoula on Highway 93. Turn west on Highway 12. Drive four miles and turn left on Mormon Peak Road. This is a good gravel road. Drive 8.7 miles to the switchback on the left where a trailhead sign is located. The sign is for "Lolo Peak Trail 1311". There is adequate parking for about six to eight cars here.

Trail Description. A trail junction and signs are located three-quarters of a mile up the trail. This junction is with the Mill Creek Trail which branches to the right.

The trail is very good. It is wide and smooth and climbs steadily, but gradually, up the ridge. For the first two miles the trail is mostly located in a heavily forested area. Then it enters an area with more widely spaced trees. Glimpses through the trees reveal the rugged north ridge of Lolo Peak located very close to the trail. I hiked this trail in late September and at that time the alpine larch were at their golden best. A truly stunning setting.

At the summit of Carlton Ridge is a sign "Carlton Ridge Elevation 8,252". A rocky spire 600 feet beyond the Carlton Ridge sign offers an excellent viewpoint to gaze at Lolo Peak above and the east ridge leading to the peak.

To reach Carlton Lake, follow the unsigned trail down past the vista point. This is a good trail that switchbacks down the ridge for about a half mile where it joins an old bulldozer road. Follow the road to the right another half mile to Carlton Lake. The lake is located in an alpine setting. A large irrigation dam detracts from the lovely scenery on the east end. The lake is about one-third mile long and about 200 yards wide.

An old trail crosses the dam and leads about one-quarter mile south to Little Carlton Lake, a very small pothole lake. The same trail can be followed for another 1.5 miles (first to the south, then west) to North One Horse Lake and Reed Lake. Both are located at the base of Lolo Peak.

To reach Lolo Peak (elevation 9,096 feet) follow the long ridge that climbs from Carlton Lake up to the peak. There is no trail. However you can use the ridge just to the south of Carlton Lake. It's about two miles from Carlton Lake to the peak.

Topographic Map. Carlton Lake.

7. Sweeney Ridge

This is a scenic and popular out-and-back hike. Many people from around Missoula use the Peterson Lake area. It often is used heavily on summer weekends, but the hike is a pleasant one. The trail starts high on a ridge and offers sensational views of Sweeney Canyon and the surrounding peaks. It is an excellent day hike for persons in good condition, or an easy overnight trek for backpackers. Use is heavy.

Distances: See Map #1
Spring 2
Peterson Lake 5

Trailhcad Directions. Diive south from Missoula to Florence on Highway 93. Continue past Florence for 1.5 miles, then turn right (west) onto the Sweeney Creek Road. Where the paved road swings left (south), keep to the right and follow the gravel road to the first junction, about 1.4 miles from Highway 93. Turn right at this junction; the sign points to "Sweeney Creek Ridge." Drive another 5.7 miles to the trailhead, which is identified by a sign. The last mile of the road is very rough. The trailhead has parking room for about ten cars and a wide place to turn around.

Trail Description. The trail, well marked and easy to follow, climbs steadily for about two miles and is steep in places. It follows Sweeney Ridge and offers an outstanding view of Sweeney Creek, the surrounding peaks, and the upper cirque. There is no water for the first two miles. At the first creek is a crude campsite. Farther on, the trail drops into Peterson Lake. The fishing here is good and a few campsites are available at the lake's upper end.

More lakes lie beyond Peterson. Visitors should try to schedule enough time to hike up to Duffy and Holloway Lakes. The scenery is well worth the extra effort.

Duffy Lake (elevation 7,330) can be reached by following the trail around the north side of Peterson Lake. The trail leads west about two miles to a cirque which contains Duffy Lake. The remains of an old irrigation dam can be seen here. Holloway Lake (elevation 7,796) lies above Duffy Lake and about one-half mile south.

The trail to Duffy and Holloway Lakes - which sit just below the main crest of the Bitterroots - steadily climbs the canyon on switchbacks. It leads past waterfalls and views of the peaks. Mountain goats inhabit the steep, rocky slopes above these two upper lakes, and the ridges are excellent for day hikes. No marked trails exist here. There is a small log structure between these upper lakes.

Mills Lake is a small lake just west of Holloway Lake. To reach it, walk around the north end of Holloway Lake and go about 100 yards west. Mills Lake sits directly beneath a sheer rock face.

Topographic Maps. Dick Creek; Carlton Lake.

8. Little St. Joseph Peak

The trail for this hike is poorly maintained and in places is hard to follow. This is a difficult hike, not recommended for the novice. The views from the top make this hike well worth the effort. Use is light.

Distance: See Map #1

Trailhead Directions. From Florence, drive 4 miles south on Highway 93 to Bass Creek Road. Turn west (right) and follow the sign pointing to "Charles Waters Campground." Drive west for two miles to the campground, staying on the paved road that skirts the campground's north side. The pavement ends at a trailhead at the west end of the campground. Drive past Bass Creek trailhead and follow road 1136 up the mountain. The switch-backed route to the road's end is seven miles in length. Take the left fork at the junction 1.2 miles up the mountain. The end of the road is just a wide turnaround; it has no signs or facilities.

Trail Description. To find the trail, walk south toward the canyon rim. The trail climbs up the mountain in a generally westerly direction. It follows the ridge crest along the north wall of Bass Creek Canyon and offers a good view of the canyon and of high rocky, jagged peaks just to the south. The course climbs steeply, winding through widely spaced trees. The trail is marked with old blazes but is poorly maintained (or perhaps not at all). Numerous tree roots could trip the careless hiker.

No water is available for the first three miles, but then thirsty hikers can listen for a stream only a few minutes' walk to the right of the trail. In places this trail is hard to follow. When in doubt, just stick to the ridge crest and continue uphill toward the peak. Above the timberline watch for rock cairns marking the path. When the trail disappears, the peak is in full view, and hikers can just climb up a fairly steep, open slope to the summit at 9,000 feet. The total elevation gain from the trailhead is about 3,000 feet.

From the top there are sensational views of jagged peaks to the south and of the Bitterroot Valley to the east. The spectacular view to the west of St. Joseph Peak is attainable from nowhere else. A ridge stretches to St. Joseph Peak from this point. This trail is not recommended for the novice. It is a demanding hike, very steep in places with uncertain footing. There is no clearly defined trail for the last mile.

Topographic Maps. St. Joseph Peak; St. Mary Peak.

9. Larry Creek Trails

The Larry Creek Trail Complex offers a varied selection of trails in an attractive forested area in the rolling foothills adjacent to the Bass Creek Campground. The area is situated at low elevations and may be used on a year-round basis. In recent years I have seen increasing winter use by snowshoers and cross country skiers, as well as by wintertime hikers. The complex consists of 4 loop trails, a picnic area, and a special group camping area. Refer to Map # 1. Also see area map at trailhead.

The Trails Are:
Fitness Trail..0.4 mile
Nature Trail ....0.5 mile
Fire Ecology Trail... 2.5 miles
Bass Day Use Trail.. 6.5 miles

Trailhead Directions. Take US-93 to Bass Creek Road 4 miles south of Florence. Drive 2 miles west and turn right on Forest Road 1316. At the turn off is a sign with a trail map. There are several parking slots next to the sign and more parking in the picnic area just west of the sign. In addition there is a large day use parking area about 300 yards north on Road 1316. The picnic area is equipped with a toilet and running water is available in season.

Trail Descriptions:
The Fitness Trail (0.4 mile) starts next to the picnic area. It consists of a short, smooth loop with several exercise stations. It is located in a parklike grove of widely spaced trees.

The Charles Waters Nature Trail (0.5 mile) starts just across Forest Road 1316 from the Fitness Trail. It winds through a forested area close to the creek. A self-guided tour utilizes signs to identify plants and trees. Specific examples include " Western Larch, Silver

Birch, Bracken, Fern, and Ocean Spray." This is an easy and pleasant hike, especially well suited to children.

The Larry Creek Fire Ecology Trail starts at the sign just across the road from the day use parking area. A pamphlet for the tour is available in the Day Use Parking Area. Because there are a number of intersecting and overlapping trails you should use the diamond shaped trail markers attached to the trees to guide you. The red diamonds mark the Fire Ecology Trail and the yellow diamonds are for the Bass Day Use Trail. The two trails overlap for about 2 miles so you will see both markers at the start and finish. The Fire Ecology Trail travels 2.5 miles through mostly easy terrain. The route leads through upland forests, past aspen groves and along a creek. The self-guided tour examines the effects of fire upon the forest and its inhabitants. The Fire Ecology Trail meanders through a park like area, climbing through widely spaced conifers. A bench is located in a convenient spot offering an exceptionally nice view of the Bitterroot Valley below and the Sapphire Mountains to the east. The trail gains about 300 feet of elevation before it diverges from the Bass Day Use Trail at a signed junction, 1.3 miles from the trailhead. The route then descends a steep wooded draw parallel to Larry Creek and then crosses the road to follow a wooded path that returns to the Day Use Parking Area.

Bass Day Use Trail (BDU) is a 6.5 mile loop trail beginning and ending at the Day Use Parking Area. The loop trail is identical to the Fire Ecology Trail for the first 1.3 miles. Just cross the road from the Day Use Parking area and look for the trail sign. The BDU Trail is marked with yellow diamonds fastened to the trees, and the Fire Ecology Trail is marked with red diamonds, consequently you will see both red and yellow markers for the first segment of each trail.

The BDU Trail meanders through a park like area climbing gradually through widely spaced conifers. At 1 mile a bench is available with a nice view of the Bitterroot valley and of the Sapphire Mountains to the east. At 1.3 miles the BDU Trail leaves the Fire Ecology Trail at a signed junction and descends into a thickly wooded draw to cross Larry Creek on a good stock bridge, then climbs again into an open upland forest. At 2 miles the trail crosses Road # 1316 and then climbs a moderately steep segment. After crossing the road the route passes several divergent trails, so watch for the yellow markers. At 2.5 miles the route passes a confusing junction with no yellow markers in sight, stay left and watch for the black rubber water bars on the trail. The trail with the rubber water bars is the BDU Trail.

The route reaches a high point at 3.2 miles. My GPS read 4,280' here, for a total elevation gain of about 800' from the trailhead. At 3.6 miles there is a sharp switchback where the trail changes direction. Watch for the yellow diamond, (the other trail is marked by blue diamonds). At 4.2 miles you reach another trail junction. Take the left fork which is marked with a yellow diamond. After a gradual descent the route reaches a series of fenced meadows. The forest changes to include cottonwood and aspen trees. The route crosses several small irrigation ditches before rejoining the Fire Ecology Trail just south of the Larry Creek Group Camping Area. The trail then returns to the Day Use Parking Area at 6.5 miles.

The Stevensville Ranger District of the Bitterroot National Forest is to be commended for their creative efforts in developing the Larry Creek Trails. These low altitude trails provide excellent outdoor recreational opportunities.

10. Bass Creek

The Bass Creek portion of this hike features easy grades and excellent campsites. The dam area at Bass Lake is rather unsightly, but otherwise the scenery along this hike is quite good, especially at the lake's south end. There are no bass swimming in Bass Lake. The lake and creek were named for an early settler in the Stevensville area. Use is heavy.

Distances (from Bass Creek trailhead): See Map #1
Old log dam on Bass Creek 1½
Bass Lake 7
Trail junction to South Fork Lolo Creek 8

Trailhead Directions. Take US-93 to Bass Creek Road 4 miles south of Florence. Drive 2.5 miles to the trailhead at the west end of the campground. All used campground facilities are available including stock facilities and ample parking space.

Trail Description. The Bass Creek trail follows an old roadbed except for a 2.5 mile section. The path climbs steadily throughout. Numerous picnic spots and heavily used campsites crowd the first two miles. There is an old log dam at about 1.5 miles. At two miles the trail starts climbing a steep switchbacked section. The trail continues along the north wall of the canyon all the way to Bass Lake. As the hiker climbs toward Bass Lake, a delightful view of the upper Bass Creek Canyon appears, revealing some excellent camping areas in clearings along the creek below.

Throughout most of its length, the trail follows an old road. This road was constructed with a bulldozer and provided access for the heavy equipment necessary to rebuild the earthen dam at Bass Lake in the early 1950s and again in 1996.

Just below the lake the view deteriorates: a raw, ugly scar marks the site of earth-moving activity that was necessary to build the large dam. A steep climb up the final 200 yards puts the hiker on the top of the earth-filled dam and reveals the long expanse of Bass Lake, its upper end framed by snowfields and sheer rock cliffs, its lower end defaced by the dam and the stark nakedness of the dead trees along its margin (a result of the extreme drawdown of the lake for irrigation use in late summer). A great many rocks and boulders crowd the lakeshore, and few flat, open spots are available for campsites.

The trail crosses the slope on the north side of the lake. About halfway around the lake another trail branches to the right and switchbacks up the steep ridge. This trail goes to the South Fork of Lolo Creek (see South Fork Lolo Creek to Bass Creek). The trail continues around the north side of the lake and then swings to the south around the west end of the lake. From here the trail has been abandoned and is no longer maintained. This wide end of Bass Lake offers striking scenery.

Topographic Maps. St. Joseph Peak; St. Mary Peak.

11. Kootenai Creek

The Kootenai Creek trail offers a moderate hike along a very picturesque creek. During the summer the Kootenai area sees heavy use, including moderate to heavy horse traffic. There are not too many good campsites, and the area is likely to be crowded during peak use periods such as holidays and long weekends. Some striking scenery may be viewed along this trail. Use is heavy.

Distances (from Kootenai Creek trailhead): See Map #1
Middle Kootenai Lakes 9½
North Kootenai Lake....................................10
South Kootenai Lake ....9 ½

Trailhead Directions. Drive south on Highway 93 from Missoula. The Kootenai Creek Road begins 6.5 miles south of Florence (about one mile north of the Stevensville junction). It is marked with a Forest Service sign. Turn right (west) at the sign and drive two miles to the trailhead parking area. The road is good, but the last one-half mile is bumpy. The trailhead has a horse loading ramp and parking space for about fifteen cars. Parking usually is inadequate for the heavy use the area receives.

Trail Description. The trail closely follows the north side of the creek. There is a small irrigation diversion dam at one-quarter mile. The trail's first two to three miles afford a delightful walk along a picturesque mountain stream. However, this lower segment is heavily used by campers, rock climbers, day hikers, fishermen, and horseback riders. Local high-schoolers consider this stretch a prime spot for beer parties. There are numerous overly-used campsites along this portion of the creek.

At about 6.5 miles the trail winds through a relatively flat area that is heavily overgrown with huckleberry bushes. For about one-half mile the site offers excellent huckleberry picking in season.

To reach the Kootenai Lakes (about 6,200 feet elevation), the hiker proceeds on the main trail (left fork). The trail starts climbing just past the flat, traversing steep switchbacks. About a mile of huffing and puffing rewards hikers with an excellent vista of the surrounding countryside. Near the top of the headwall the trail crosses the creek and reaches a junction. The right fork goes about one-half mile to North Kootenai Lake.

The left fork leads to Middle Kootenai Lake, however, you must first cross the outlet stream below the lakes. This is a deep ford. From Middle Kootenai Lake you can climb the switchbacks and follow the trail to South Kootenai Lake.

There actually are two Middle Kootenai Lakes - a larger body lies about one-quarter mile west of the first. To reach the bigger lake, follow the north shore of the first lake, then make the short walk west. These lakes are located in an attractive glacial bowl

Topographic Maps. St. Joseph Peak; St. Mary Peak.

12. St. Mary Peak

This out-and-back hike is popular but it is more rigorous than many others since it involves an appreciable elevation gain. The climb is worthwhile, though, for the spectacular long-distance views that are available from the top. An old fire lookout tower is located at the summit. Use is moderate.

Distances: See Map #2
Spring ....*¼*
St. Mary summit ....*4 ½*

Trailhead Directions. Drive south from Missoula on Highway 93. Indian Prairie Road is four miles south of the Stevensville turnoff, and marked by a US Forest Service sign. Turn right on Indian Prairie Road and follow it for about nine miles to the trailhead. The trailhead area has room for about fifteen cars and has a toilet.

Trail Description. The trail to St. Mary Peak is well marked and clearly defined. The climb, however, is more strenuous than many people expect: the elevation gain from the trailhead to the top is approximately 2,500 feet. The trail ascends steadily throughout its length. It starts to climb immediately, switchbacking through the trees for the first 1.5 miles. At about one-quarter mile, fifty feet left of the trail, there is a spring which features benches and a horse trough. Hikers should fill their water bottles here.

The trail steadily climbs the south face of the ridge that runs up to St. Mary Peak. At about two miles, a side path forks to the left (south). This fork takes hikers down a steep gradient to the McCalla Lakes. These two small, shallow lakes lie in the canyon to the left of the main trail, about one-half mile south of the junction. The trail to the lakes is poor.

The main trail to St. Mary Peak continues along the ridge face. There are benches to rest on at a few locations. At about 2.5 miles the trail starts to switchback tortuously across the bare rock face of the ridge. The course is easy to follow and the mountain top remains in view at all times. The summit, at 9,350 feet, offers a splendid view of the surrounding Bitterroot peaks, the valley, and the Sapphire range to the east.

The summit of St. Mary Mountain is the site of a spindly US Forest Service fire control tower.

The three rest stops along the trail were built by Father Ravalli Council of the Knights of Columbus. Each year this Catholic organization sponsors a religious pilgrimage to St. Mary Peak. The event generally begins early on a Sunday morning in mid-August. Participants gather at St. Mary's Mission in Stevensville, then drive to the trailhead. From there they walk to the peak together. They stop at each of the three rest areas for a brief religious service and then celebrate mass at the top. A wide range of people participates in this event: some are in their mid-seventies; some are children who are so small their parents must carry them. Additional information about this ceremony is available from the St. Mary's church in Stevensville.

Topographic Map. St. Mary Peak.

13. Big Creek to Bear Creek

The main trail to the primary destination, Big Creek Lake, is easy walking for all but the last one-half mile. Big Creek Lake is the largest of the high Bitterroot lakes and is one of the most scenic. It offers numerous good campsites with excellent views. Other trails to smaller nearby lakes make good day hikes for persons camping at Big Creek Lake. The trail into Idaho and back to Montana, over two passes, features a variety of scenic splendors as well as a chance to see wildlife. A few portions of this interior segment are difficult going; yet the scenery and the chance for solitude should make the effort more than worthwhile (see also Bear Creek). Use is moderate to Big Creek Lake and light beyond.

Distances (from Big Creek trailhead): See Map #2

Big Flat *5½*
Trail junction to South Fork Big Creek lakes *8½*
South Fork Lake *11*
Pearl Lake *12*
Big Creek Lake *9*
Unnamed lake above Big Creek Lake *12*
Packbox Pass *13*
White Sand Lake *18*
Bear Creek Pass *20*
Bryan Lake *22*
Bear Creek trailhead *30*

Trailhead Directions. Big Creek end. From the Stevensville junction, drive 5.5 miles south on Highway 93 to the Big Creek Road (a Forest Service sign marks the turnoff). Turn west (right) and follow the signs to the Big Creek trailhead, four miles from Highway 93. This road crosses an ugly open-pit mine at about three miles. After passing the old mine, the road climbs gradually to a junction. Take the right fork down toward the creek. At the trailhead are a small campground, a horse ramp, and adequate parking.

Bear Creek end. From Victor, drive 3.3 miles south on Highway 93 to Bear Creek Road, also marked by a sign for "Bear Creek Trail." Turn right and go 2.2 miles west. Then turn right (north) on Red Crow Road and drive .7 mile. At a road junction turn left and drive three miles west to Bear Creek trailhead.

Trail Description. This well-maintained trail starts on the south side of Big Creek. At about one and one-quarter miles it crosses to the north bank on an excellent bridge sturdy enough for horse use. For the first five miles the trail runs on a fairly level grade and offers numerous camps, some right next to the creek. The creek is very attractive, with many wide pools and clean, white sandbars. The walking is quite easy, but the trail shows evidence of very heavy horse traffic.

At about five and one-half miles the hiker reaches a large, open, flat area with some very large house sized boulders. This is the Big Flat camping area, a popular and overly used camp site. After leaving the Big Flat area, the trail enters a narrow canyon and begins a steeper ascent. Here the creek is compressed between steep rock walls, and rushes and roars with power. Rocky spires tower above. Then the trail enters heavy forest again, climbing more gently. A log bridge crosses the creek at about seven miles, then the trail starts a gradual switchbacked climb up toward the canyon headwall. At 8.5 miles a Forest Service sign marks the trail junction to the South Fork Lake.

South Fork Lake lies about 2.5 miles south of the junction along a very poor trail. The path runs through heavy timber for the first mile, then along an open slope above the South Fork of Big Creek. The last one-half mile to the lake is a steep climb. South Fork Lake is a high, isolated lake surrounded by steep, bare, rocky walls on three sides and by heavy forest at its lower end. It is one of the Bitterroot's more isolated lakes, and it receives very few visitors.

28

There are a few good campsites at the lower end. It features good fishing - as well as a lot of mosquitoes in season.

Pearl Lake may be reached by following the poorly defined trail around the west side of South Fork Lake, then up the open slope to the north for about three-quarters of a mile. (Do not mistake the small pothole lake about halfway up the slope for Pearl Lake.) Pearl Lake sits in a high glacial cirque in a truly alpine setting, surrounded by bare, rocky walls. A few trees and a relatively flat area near the outlet on its east end provide a good camping area.

Big Creek Lake is one-half mile past the South Fork junction, along the right fork over steep switchbacks. The trail emerges at a new (1979) concrete dam, about ten feet high and twenty feet across. The dam appears somewhat out of place, although dam construction here left few scars: helicopters were used to fly in premixed concrete, and the dam site was not as badly disturbed as those of so many other Bitterroot high lakes.

The trail continues across the dam and around the west shore of the lake. Now the splendor of Big Creek Lake reveals itself. This is the largest of all the high Bitterroot lakes. It sits in a large, high-mountain valley and is surrounded by steep rock faces and towering, jagged peaks. Waterfalls cascade down the south wall. Big Creek Lake was formerly two lakes: the raised water level created by the dam joined them at a narrow section.

Campsites are found along the north shore of the lake at many locations, including one site very close to the dam. Almost all the camping spots are in the open and provide an excellent view of the lake and surrounding peaks. The fishing is good here and there are some good routes over which campers may make day hikes.

Another high lake can be reached via a steep trail west of Big Creek Lake. The small lake nests among the high peaks on a shelf about one mile west of the larger lake. To reach it, walk on the trail for about two-thirds of the distance around Big Creek Lake. About one-quarter mile beyond the narrowest part of the lake (about two miles from the dam), one fork of a trail junction (marked by a small rock pile) heads to the right (west). This poorly defined trail leads up a steep, open slope for one mile to the unnamed, isolated lake. It is a very lovely place and is surrounded by sheer rock cliffs. There are a few campsites at the lower end. This is a good alternative for those who may feel that Big Creek Lake is too crowded.

To reach Packbox Pass from Big Creek Lake, continue around the lake on the main trail. This is the trail that starts on the north side of Big Creek Lake near the dam and follows the shore of the lake around to its south or upper end. Here the trail starts a gradual, switchbacked ascent. It winds through a landscape of widely spaced trees, large boulders, and lots of huckleberry bushes. There are ever-changing views of the lake below and the peaks towering above. The switchbacks traverse rock ledges polished to a smooth finish by the abrasive action of ancient glaciers. Snowfields linger here on the north-facing slopes even in August, and tracks in the soft mud of the trail attest to the passage of moose, elk, and mountain goats.

At the top of Packbox Pass some very unusual, jagged rocky spires appear to the south. The trail then begins a long, steady descent into a thickly timbered, swampy valley on the Idaho side. The trail descends through wide, marshy meadows, heavy brush, and (in July and August) clouds of swarming mosquitoes. The trail follows Packbox Creek and offers a perspective quite different from that on the east side of the range. Few high, jagged peaks can be seen after the first mile of descent, and the view is mostly of a long, heavily timbered valley. Large, open meadows with high grass and lots of brush provide ideal habitat for large game animals. There are numerous horse camps along the trail. The trail junction to White Sand Lake is about three miles below the pass. The fork is marked by a large blaze on a tree, and the trail, which follows the creek to its origins at White Sand Lake, is well defined. The trail runs through brush up a steep slope and across a swampy area for about two miles. White Sand Lake, surrounded by heavy forest, is characterized by white, sandy shores and several large sand bars. The area is marshy and moose can be seen here in the summer. They often browse in the lake, feeding on aquatic vegetation with their heads underwater. There are a few good campsites here, and a comfortable camp can be made right on the soft sand of the beach. This lake does not get many visitors.

Bear Creek Pass can be reached by following the Packbox Creek trail downstream from the White Sand Lake trail junction for about one-quarter mile. The fork to Bear Creek Pass is marked by an old Forest Service sign high on a tree. The trail heads in a generally easterly direction toward Bryan Lake. The distance to the top of Bear Creek Pass is only about 3.5 miles, but the trail is rough and very steep, gaining about 3,000 feet from the trail junction at Packbox Creek. The trail is poorly defined after the first mile, where it emerges from the forest and crosses bare rock faces. Watch for cairns. The view improves with elevation. At about three miles the trail swings sharply south. It goes through a draw, then crosses a late lingering snowfield. The last one-half mile to the top of Bear Creek Pass is quite steep.

At the point where the course swings south to the pass it is very easy to lose the main trail: another trail, old and poorly defined, heads northeast aiming directly at the top of the ridge. This is a pleasant detour but it is not the main trail. This path traverses high, open meadows for about one-quarter mile, and leads to a cliff overlooking South Fork Lake. There are some excellent isolated campsites here with unusually attractive views. The jagged spires of Sky Pilot Peak rise immediately to the southeast and seem almost close enough to touch.

To reach Bryan Lake and the Bear Creek trailhead, follow the trail back into Montana over Bear Creek Pass. Bryan Lake lies about 1.5 miles from the top of Bear Creek Pass. The trail descends across bare, rocky slopes. The entire upper end of this high canyon is decorated by silver-grey trees left by an old forest fire. The dead trees and steep, rocky slopes fashion an eerie landscape through which the trail gradually descends. Bryan Lake nestles below in a long, narrow, steep-walled canyon. Follow the trail downhill for 8.5 miles to the Bear Creek trailhead. (For details on Bryan Lake and the trail down Bear Creek, see Bear Creek Trail.)

Topographic Maps. Victor; Gash Point; White Sand Lake.

14. Glen Lake and Hidden Lake

The short walk to Glen Lake is an easy day hike, good for a Sunday stroll in the mountains. It has some nice campsites and is an excellent place to take a youngster on a first hike or a first overnight hike. Hidden Lake is lightly used, and reaching it demands a more vigorous hike over a poorly defined trail. Hidden Lake has potential for an isolated camping experience and good fishing but lacks a good view. The area is somewhat swampy, and mosquitoes abound in season. Use to Glen Lake is moderate, very light to Hidden Lake.

Distances: See Map #2
Glen Lake *2½*
Unnamed lake north of Glen Lake *2¾*
Hidden Lake *5*

Trailhead Directions. Drive south on Highway 93 to Big Creek turnoff, 5.5 miles south of the Stevensville junction and about 1.5 miles north of Victor. A US Forest Service sign marks the road.

Follow the signs toward Big Creek trailhead. The road starts to climb where it crosses the open-pit mine. The ugly scar here is the remainder of the old Curlew Mine. After crossing the mine dump, the road climbs gradually for about one-half mile to a junction. The right fork here is the Big Creek trail access. The fork is clearly marked with a Forest Service sign.

To reach the Glen Lake trail, continue to the left along the Smith Creek Road (as indicated by the road sign). This road continues a gradual climb through clearcut areas, following a switchbacked course at its upper end. The Glen Lake trailhead is about six miles past the Big Creek trail turn. A Forest Service sign indicates the trailhead.

Trail Description. The trail to Glen Lake is clearly marked. Almost its entire length winds through heavy timber. The Trail is fairly easy: it gains little elevation and descends gradually for its last 100 yards to the small, shallow lake. Glen Lake nestles in a canyon, with a steep bare rock cliff on its south side and heavy timber on the north. At the lower end are several good campsites and a small, crude log cabin.

The trail to Hidden Lake is not shown on the Selway-Bitterroot Wilderness Map. To reach Hidden Lake the hiker must expend considerably more effort. The trail is poorly defined. Hidden Lake lies approximately 2.5 miles northwest of Glen Lake. It is aptly named. The hiker follows the trail along the north shore of Glen Lake to the upper end, then turns right and climbs the steep path that winds along the creek. One can follow this creek to its source at a small, shallow lake about one-quarter mile north of Glen Lake, then cross this lake at its lower end. The trail runs in a westerly direction along the edge of the lake. In about one-quarter mile the path fades out where it reaches a steep ridge. By looking uphill to the left (south), hikers can locate the trail switchbacks and then can follow the trail or just go straight up the steep ridge on the left.

At the ridge top, a view of nearby jagged, rocky peaks appears to the south. Hikers should walk along the ridge to the west. Here the trail becomes well defined again. It follows the ridge crest for about two-thirds of a mile, descending gradually. Then it drops off to the right (north) in a steep series of switchbacks. Winding through the forest, it descends a steep slope to Hidden Lake, a small, deep lake at the bottom of a canyon. Only a few campsites are available here. The fishing can be very good for rainbow trout. Clouds of mosquitoes swarm about this marshy area in July and August.

Topographic Maps. Victor; Gash Point.

15. Bear Creek Overlook

This is a two and one-half mile switchbacked trail offering a gentle climb to an exceptional scenic overlook. The setting and view from Bear Creek Overlook are powerful and most dramatic and well worth the hike. Try it, you'll like it! Use is light.

Distance: See Map #2

Trailhead Directions. From Victor, drive 3.3 miles south on Highway 93 to Bear Creek Road, which is also marked by a sign for "Bear Creek Trail". Turn right and go 2.2 miles west. Turn right on Red Crow Road and drive .7 mile north. At the road junction, turn right, staying on Red Crow Road. There is a sign here indicating Bear Overlook is nine miles. About one mile past the sign, turn left at Pleasant View Drive. There is a road junction 4.1 miles past the Pleasant View Drive turn. Take the left fork. This is FS Road #1325. 3.1 miles past this junction is a "Y"-shaped junction. Take the right fork to the trailhead ½ mile beyond. The road is blocked with a gate just beyond the trailhead and there is room for six or seven cars here.

Trail Description. The trail starts climbing immediately. There are many switchbacks and the grade is relatively easy. Throughout its 3-mile length, the trail winds through lodgepole and spruce forests with beargrass and huckleberry bushes. I hiked this trail in early September and found huckleberries on the bushes near the top.

At the summit are the picturesque remains of an old log cabin. Follow the trail to the south past the cabin and slightly downhill to the spectacular promontory. The overlook is perched on the edge of a sheer cliff face overlooking Bear Creek Canyon. It is a most dramatic setting. Green algae stains the rocks in the immediate vicinity. The wilderness is revealed below from the edge of this lofty perch. This viewpoint is unique in the Bitterroots.

Topographic Maps. Gash Point.

16. Bear Creek

This trail offers lovely scenery and good fishing access to the creek. A delightful picnic spot is located next to a lovely waterfall within easy hiking distance of the trailhead. Excellent huckleberry picking is common in season. For the more energetic, a 8.5 mile hike to Bryan Lake provides exceptional scenery and good fishing.

For the even more ambitious, the trek to Bryan Lake may serve as one leg of a longer point-to-point hike over two mountain passes into the Big Creek drainage (see Big Creek to Bear Creek). The first three miles is heavily used.

Distances: See Map #2

Waterfall and Picnic Spot *1½*
Trail junction to South Fork Bear Creek *3½*
Trail junction to Bear Lake *5¾*
Bear Lake *8½*
Bryan Lake (old burn area) *8½*

Trailhead Directions. From Victor, drive 3.3 miles south on Highway 93 to Bear Creek Road, which also is marked by a sign for "Bear Creek Trail." Turn right and go 2.2 miles west. Then turn right on Red Crow Road and drive .7 mile north. At a road junction turn left and drive three miles west to Bear Creek trailhead.

Trail Description. The Bear Creek trail starts on an easy grade that follows the creek on its south side. The trail offers good access to the creek, which has numerous wide pools and at 1.5 miles there is a lovely waterfall. The lower two or three miles are a favorite fishing area for many locals. At three miles the trail crosses to the north bank of the creek. This can be a difficult crossing in high water, but is a pleasant interlude on a hot August day.

An interesting side hike is available on the South Fork of Bear Creek. At about 3.5 miles the trail junction to the South Fork of Bear Creek is reached. This unsigned junction is about one-quarter mile past the first crossing. The trail crosses Bear Creek and heads up the South Fork. This can be a difficult crossing. This trail is poorly maintained and hard to find. It climbs steeply in places through dense forest. There is an excellent campsite about half a mile up the trail. The trail continues beyond the campsite for about three miles.

For the determined (stubborn) hiker it is possible to continue up the South Fork for about four more miles to Two Lakes. The trail does not go all the way to Two Lakes, and a compass and map are required. Two Lakes is located in a high cirque surrounded by bare rock walls and jagged ridges. This picturesque spot is very rarely visited. The remains of an old unused irrigation dam may be viewed at Two Lakes.

Another possible side hike is to Bear Lake, which can be reached by following the main Bear Creek trail beyond the South Fork trail junction for about two-and-one-quarter miles. Hikers should then watch for the North Fork of Bear Creek - the first sizable tributary joining Bear Creek from the north (right). A very poor trail leads north to Bear Lake. This trail has not been maintained for years and is hard to follow.

Bryan Lake is only two miles upstream from the North Fork junction along the main trail of Bear Creek. The trail climbs steeply at times and is rough in places in these last two miles. Bryan Lake lies in a high glacial valley. The landscape is eerie: the lake is surrounded by dead grey trees killed years ago by a forest fire. On the south side of the lake, sheer rock cliffs rise toward high peaks. There are a few campsites at the lake's lower end, and good fishing for fat cutthroats. For those who seek a longer point-to-point hike, the trail continues beyond Bryan Lake to Bear Creek Pass and then to Packbox Pass and Big Creek. (For details, see Big Creek to Bear Creek.)

Topographic Maps. Victor; Gash Point; White Sand Lake.

17. Fred Burr Creek to Mill Creek

Fred Burr Canyon has been closed to public access for a number of years. In 1995 the Forest Service negotiated access through private land at the mouth of Fred Burr. A new trailhead was built in the fall of 1995. The trail leading through Fred Burr Canyon follows Fred Burr Creek for about 4.5 miles to Fred Burr Reservoir on an old jeep road. The hike is very pleasant and the road climbs at an easy grade. There are several nice pools with good fishing access. The upper section of Fred Burr Creek between the reservoir and Fred Burr Lake is very scenic. The area above Fred Burr Lake along the crest of the Bitterroots is magnificent alpine country. An excellent point-to-point hike is available by hiking over the ridge above Fred Burr Lake and then hiking down Mill Creek Canyon to the trailhead there.

Distances: See Map #3

Fred Burr Reservoir...*4½*
Fred Burr Lake *12*
Pass into Mill Creek Canyon..........................*13*
Lockwood Lake *13½*
Mill Lake...*15*
Mill Creek Trailhead......................................*26*

Trailhead Directions. From Victor, drive south on Highway 93 for 3.5 miles to Bear Creek Road, marked by a sign. Turn right (west) and follow the pavement 2.4 miles to a T in the road. Turn left and drive 1.2 miles south, where the road turns west and heads directly toward Fred Burr Canyon. Do not follow the paved main road where it turns south; instead continue west on the gravel road toward the mouth of Fred Burr Canyon for another 1.7 miles on Fred Burr Road and follow the signs to the trailhead.

Trail Description. From the trailhead the trail starts downhill almost immediately. It winds through a wooded area for about one-half mile before joining a road that follows the creek all the way to Fred Burr Reservoir. This lower end of the canyon is private property and there are a few cabins hidden in the trees close to the creek. The road continues on private property for about one mile before reaching a locked gate and National Forest sign.

The trail climbs at a moderate grade gaining about 1,000 feet in the 4.5 miles from the trailhead to the reservoir. The jeep road makes for easy walking. Several spots offer easy access for fishing in wide pools in the creek. The very steep canyon walls tower to the north. The trail traverses an area where fires burned most of the trees. There is a bridge across the creek below the reservoir. The jeep road ends just past the bridge at the reservoir and the trail continues along the north side.

Fred Burr Reservoir (about 5,100 feet elevation) is about one-third mile long. Its lower end is blocked with an irrigation dam and a steel irrigation control mechanism. There are several campsites around the lake; one is located close to the dam. The trail crosses the creek just above the upper end of the reservoir.

Fred Burr Lake is located about seven miles upstream at 7,448 feet elevation. The trail follows the creek closely for most of that distance, crossing and recrossing it four times. The trail is dim and a little hard to find in places, especially where it crosses open meadows. Watch for old tree blazes and rock cairns to help find the trail. Because it follows the creek closely, there is little danger of getting very lost. The canyon above the reservoir is mostly open meadows. A great many of the trees were burned in the 1988 fires.

About four miles above the reservoir, the trail changes from its westerly direction and turns south to enter upper Fred Burr Canyon. This is wild and rugged country at the headwaters of Fred Burr Creek, and the trail runs through a deep, glaciated canyon. In places the sheer rock walls tower at least 2,000 feet above the canyon's floor. The trail to Fred Burr Lake follows the creek through heavy forest, then starts climbing steeply on the western wall of the canyon.

Fred Burr, a small, high-mountain lake, is a lovely green jewel lying just below a sheer rock wall. It sits above the thick, dark-green forest in the basin below.

The trail to Mill Creek crosses the dam at Fred Burr Lake, then climbs very steeply up the west wall of the canyon. The trail switchbacks across an open face of the canyon wall to an overlook about 500 feet above the lake. From there it ascends at a more gradual rate toward the ridge to the south, traversing some lovely alpine meadows which lie just below the crest of the Bitterroot Mountains. There are several excellent and very scenic campsites along here.

The trail crosses to Mill Creek Canyon on a high ridge (about 8,000 feet). From the ridgetop the entire expanse of upper Fred Burr Canyon is revealed, and the scene to the north in Mill Creek Canyon is equally captivating. Immediately below the ridge nestles Lockwood Lake, a lovely lake high on a rock shelf at the head of Mill Creek Canyon. Below are two more lakes: Heinrich Lake lies just one-quarter mile below Lockwood, and Mill Lake is about 2.5 miles below and south of Heinrich.

The trail descends the rocky, open face above and north of Lockwood Lake. Then it crosses the abandoned dam and descends further along the open slope to Heinrich Lake. From there it switchbacks through open, huckleberry-bushed slopes to a junction and Mill Creek trail.

The trail junction is marked with a sign. The trail to the right (west) leads to Mill Lake, about one-quarter mile upstream. To the left, the trail follows Mill Creek east to the Mill Canyon trailhead, about eleven miles downstream. For more details on Mill Canyon and its lakes, see Mill Creek Trail.

Topographic Maps. Blodgett Mountain; Printz Ridge; Hamilton North.

18. Sheafman Creek

This out-and-back trail may be used either for an excellent day hike or as a very easy overnighter. It receives only light use. The trail is good, the scenery is beautiful, and some excellent campsites are available. An exceptional choice for beginning hikers, this course is a really good place to take a youngster on his or her first overnight camp.

Distances: See Map #3

Sheafman Lake *6*
Knaack Lake *6½*
Aichele Lake *6¾*

Trailhead Directions. From Hamilton drive 5 miles north on US-93. Turn west at the traffic light onto Dutch Hill Road. Drive 3 miles west and turn right at the T junction. Follow the paved road another mile to West Cow Creek Road. Turn left and follow this good gravel road uphill 4.9 miles to the trailhead. A wide spot in the road provides room to park 6-8 cars, no sign or other facilities are available.

Trail Description. The trail starts high on the south wall of Sheafman Canyon. An old skid road provides a level path for the first quarter mile. The trail then forks off to the west. It climbs a moderate grade in heavy forest with slight dips and rises for two miles. Then it drops slightly into the creek bottom to cross the stream. There is a crude campsite near the stream crossing at about three miles. The creek crossing usually requires wading. Crossing the creek several times, the trail climbs moderately for its remaining length to lower Sheafman Lake. After the second creek crossing located about four miles upstream, the trail passes through some wet and muddy areas.

Sheafman Lake, in a glacial cirque at 7,165 feet, is a delightful spot. Sheer rock walls ascend to the ridge tops. One beach is relatively flat and offers excellent campsites. A small irrigation dam controls the lake's outflow.

To reach Knaack Lake, at 7,495 feet, follow the trail upstream from the head of Sheafman Lake. There are some cairns marking the trail. This is a rather steep one-half mile ascent. Knaack Lake lies at the base of a sheer rock face decorated with snowfields and waterfalls. It offers prime campsites and beautiful scenery. Visitors can scramble up the low ridge at the head of the lake for a view of the next drainage and an exciting vista of the high surrounding peaks.

Tiny Aichele Lake can be found among rocky cliffs above and to the west of Knaack Lake.

Topographic Maps. Printz Ridge; Hamilton North.

19. Mill Creek

Mill Creek offers considerable variety. The lower end features towering rock walls on the canyon's north side and a charming waterfall, complete with a swimming hole. As you climb further up the canyon, there is some exceptional alpine scenery, especially in the area close to Heinrich and Lockwood Lakes and the ridge leading to Fred Burr Lake. The fires of 2000 burned the lower 4.5 miles of Mill Creek. The first ½ mile is not so bad, but the next 4 miles is badly blackened, although some of the area near the creek is still green. For example, the trees near the falls are unburned.

Distances (from Mill Creek trailhead): See Map #3

Waterfalls..*3*
Trail junction to Hauf Lake..............................*5*
Hauf Lake...*7*
Trail junction to Sears Lake............................*9*
Sears lake..*10*
Mill Lake...*11*
Heinrich Lake...*12½*
Lockwood Lake...*13*
Fred Burr Lake...*14½*
Fred Burr Reservoir......................................*21½*
Fred Burr trailhead......................................*26½*

Trailhead Directions. From Missoula, drive about forty miles south on Highway 93 to Woodside (which is about five miles north of Hamilton). At the traffic light, turn right on Dutch Hill Road. A Forest Service sign at this intersection points west to Mill Creek Trail No. 64. Drive west 2.2 miles on Dutch Hill Road to a junction. Turn left (south) on Bowman Road, and drive .2 mile to the trail sign, "Mill Creek Trail No. 64," Drive west .8 mile to the trailhead at a small Forest Service picnic area. The trailhead has a horse loading ramp, and ample parking.

Trail Description. An excellent trail begins along the south side of Mill Creek, a boulder-strewn, rushing mountain stream with numerous deep pools. The first one-quarter mile above the trailhead is cluttered with irrigation ditches, flumes, and headgates. The trail follows the south side of the creek for about one-half mile. Then a log bridge with handrail crosses the stream at a creekside clearing which is used as a camping area. (Avoid the left fork in the trail just before the bridge - this is a dead-end path that serves the irrigation ditch.) From the bridge, the trail follows the north side of Mill Creek for almost its entire length. The canyon is very narrow at the start of the trail but opens up considerably after the first mile. Sheer, towering rock cliffs appear on the north side, with steep, wooded slopes on the south.

At about three miles the trail winds past a lovely waterfall with a deep pool at its bottom. The waterfall is on the left where the trail emerges from the lower canyon and crosses a clearing with large, rock slabs. The pool is big enough for a quick swim - its icy waters are a delight on a hot August day.

Another deep, wide pool occurs about one-half mile further upstream. This pool also is large enough for a swim, and features a slippery rock slide. To reach the excellent camping area in a clearing on the south bank, it is necessary to cross the creek.

The Hauf Lake trail junction lies about 5 miles upstream from the Mill Creek trailhead. The Hauf Lake junction is marked by a cairn and it is not easy to find. There is a small three inch long arrow carved into a tree at the junction. Hauf Lake offers an opportunity for a side trip.

The Hauf Lake trail goes south across Mill Creek, which must be waded - there is no bridge. The trail is poorly marked and hard to follow. It first runs through heavy timber on the flat for about one-quarter mile, then starts climbing steeply through a heavily forested slope. Hauf Lake, about 2,100 feet above the trail junction and two miles away, lies in a shelf high above the canyon. This is a killer climb.

Hauf Lake is at 7.300 feet elevation, in a lovely, high basin. There is a rock irrigation dam. An old cabin and a few old out-buildings still stand.

Sears Lake offers another opportunity for a side trip. The Sears Lake trail junction is about nine miles up the Mill Creek trail, on the east end of a large clearing. It is marked by a sign. To get on the Sears Lake trail, take the south fork (to the left) for 100 yards to Mill Creek. (Some excellent campsites are available here along the creek.) The creek must be waded - there is no bridge. The trail runs through heavy timber and marshy areas for a few hundred yards, then starts to climb at a very steep pitch.

Sears Lake lies about 1.5 miles from the trail junction, in a high glacial cirque on a shelf in Mill Canyon's south wall. The lake is faced by steep rock walls on two sides and by marshy timbered terrain on a third side. Sears Lake is a very pretty lake, but an earthen irrigation dam and water-level control equipment detract somewhat from its beauty. The dam is still in regular use, as is a modern galvanized steel culvert and a large new irrigation-flow control valve. Old logs, dredged from the lake by horse power, lie in rotting piles below the dam.

Still, despite these untidy details, you can look back from the lake at magnificent views of Mill Creek Valley below and the high, jagged peaks of the valley's north wall. The lovely alpine slopes above the lake are home for mountain goats. A few campsites are located at the lower end of the lake.

To reach Mill Lake, at 6,500 feet, continue along the main trail on the north side of Mill Creek. The trail offers easy walking up a gentle grade until the last mile, which climbs more steeply toward the lake. Mill Lake lies 100 yards beyond a trail junction which is reached just before the stream crossing. This junction is marked with signs to Heinrich and Lockwood lakes. The left fork leads across Mill Creek to Mill Lake. There is one good campsite next to the creek crossing and there are several more at the lake.

Mill Lake itself is not as attractive as the scenic hike up the canyon. Located in a lovely glacial cirque, the lake is surrounded by towering cliffs on one side and thick forest on the others.

However, a large irrigation dam built of fitted stones detracts from the scenery. By late August, irrigation demands have drawn the lake quite low. Stark, muddy shores and grey, dead trees distract the eye from the beauty of the surrounding mountain peaks.

Heinrich and Lockwood Lakes offer attractive campsites only a short hike beyond Mill Lake. From Mill Lake, take the trail back across Mill Creek to the trail junction sign, and then hike north toward Heinrich Lake. The trail is steep, and it switchbacks across the rock faces north of Mill Lake. The path is well marked with cairns.

Heinrich Lake, one of the most attractive Bitterroot mountain lakes, lies about 1.5 miles from the trail junction at 7,250 feet. Man's intrusions are minimal here - a small excavation and a rusty metal culvert are the only human signs. The lake outlets at a six-foot-high stone wall. The lake is surrounded by cliffs, shiny with snow-melt in late spring. It offers a magnificent view of Mill Creek Canyon. By looking down the canyon length, you can easily discern the path carved by prehistoric glaciers. The classic glacier course is evident in the characteristic U-shaped canyon walls.

Lockwood Lake, elevation 7,445 feet, lies about one-quarter mile above Heinrich Lake. Just follow the trail across the lower end of Heinrich. Cairns mark the steep trail clearly. Lockwood Lake sits on a high, isolated rock shelf and offers another fine view of Mill Creek Canyon and Mill Lake. Its small irrigation dam is old and overgrown and unobtrusive. A few good campsites are available here.

The trail to Fred Burr Lake is a bit tricky to find, but the result is well worth the effort. First follow the trail across the bottom of Lockwood Lake. This path, marked by cairns, crosses the rock face north of Lockwood Lake on switchbacks. It runs north until it reaches the ridge crest that separates the Mill Creek and Fred Burr watersheds. Here is the tricky part of the trail: just before it reaches the ridge, the trail enters a rock chute. Watch for a cairn on the left just before the trail enters the chute. Avoid the chute, and follow the trail using the cairn as a guide. (The path that leads directly through the chute reaches a dead-end in about 100 feet, at a sheer 1,000-foot-high cliff overlooking upper Fred Burr Canyon.) The actual trail climbs another few hundred yards, traversing the rock face high above Lockwood Lake. It straddles the top of the ridge, at about 8,000 feet, then crosses to the Fred Burr side. The trail down follows the north side of the ridge, passing huge boulders and crossing high mountain meadows that are nursed by clear streams and melting snows. It is a truly delightful environment: here high alpine meadows lie near the very crest of the Bitterroot Mountains. There are several excellent campsites along here, and sometimes mountain goats and eagles can be seen.

About one-half mile past the crest, the trail starts to descend steeply to Fred Burr Lake, which can be viewed from an overlook about 500 feet above. From the overlook, the trail switchbacks down to the lake. Fred Burr Lake, elevation about 7,400 feet, is a high mountain tarn whose color is an unusual emerald green. An irrigation dam mars its otherwise pristine beauty. From here to the Fred Burr trailhead is about a twelve mile hike. See "Fred Burr" for details for the hike to this trailhead.

Topographic Maps. Blodgett Mountain; Printz Ridge; Hamilton North.

20. Blodgett Canyon to Big Sand Lake

Blodgett Canyon is one of the most picturesque and scenically varied Bitterroot Canyons. A good trail for the entire length of

Blodgett Creek offers excellent opportunities for hiking, fishing, and wildlife viewing. The trail follows Blodgett Creek upstream at a moderate grade. The hiking is relatively easy for at least the first four miles. There are excellent views of the sheer towering walls of the canyon and good access to some wide deep pools in the creek. There are some charming waterfalls located about 3.5 miles up the trail. Moose are commonly seen along the trail and mountain goats may be viewed high on the canyon's walls.

Several interesting options are available for those interested in longer hikes. A side trip to High Lake is one possibility. Another alternative is the hike to Blodgett Lake located at the head of Blodgett Creek. Still another option is to climb the steep switchbacked slope and cross Blodgett Pass into Idaho and hike to Big Sand Lake. An interesting and challenging point-to-point hike may be completed by hiking out to the Twin Lakes trailhead via the East Fork of Moose Creek. Use is heavy for the first two miles and light beyond.

Distances: See Map #4
Bridge..*3.1*
First waterfall...*4.4*
Trail junction to High Lake............................*6½*
Trail junction to Blodgett Lake....................*10½*
Blodgett Lake..*12½*
Blodgett Pass...*12*
Avalanche zone...*13-16*
Big Sand Lake..*18*
Moose Creek trail junction.........................*23½*
Moose Lake...*28½*
Twin Lakes trailhead.......................................*33*

Trailhead Directions. At the traffic light on Highway 93 in Hamilton, turn west onto Main Street and drive through town. The road crosses the bridge over the Bitterroot River. At 1.2 miles turn right (north) on Rickets Road. Drive one-half mile to Blodgett Camp Road. Turn left (west) and drive 1.4 miles. Then follow the signs to the Blodgett Canyon trailhead, and a lovely campground next to the creek in the mouth of Blodgett Canyon. There is an excellent parking area for hikers. Its facilities include toilets, picnic tables, and a horse ramp.

Trail Description. The trail starts on the south side of the creek at the mouth of Blodgett Canyon. Lower Blodgett Canyon is probably the most picturesque of the Bitterroot canyons: it is framed by high, sheer rock walls and its opening is wider than most of the other canyon entrances. The trail is excellent and well maintained. The first few miles are mostly in forest offering occasional views of the sheer, towering walls of the canyon. The grade is gradual, with few steep sections to climb. About 300 yards from the road there is a granite memorial next to the trail. At about one mile there is a nice campsite next to a wide pool on the creek. For the next four or five miles the character of the creek alternates between two extremes. In places it flows as a wide mountain stream with clear pools; in other spots it is a foaming, splashing torrent leaping over large boulders and forming deep pools below rushing waterfalls. There are some very nice fishing holes along this stretch.

The trail crosses the creek on a good bridge at 3.1 miles. There are several campsites here; some are next to the creek. The clearing offers an excellent view of the canyon to the east. Looking from the bridge, a natural stone arch can be seen on the ridge top to the south and slightly west.

At about 4.4 miles the creek flows through a narrow canyon, creating a small waterfall and deep pool below. In a parklike area on the slope above the waterfall are some excellent campsites. A second waterfall is located ½ mile upstream.

The trail junction leading to High Lake is reached at about 6.5 miles, the junction is signed. To reach High Lake follow the poorly-defined trail downstream about 100 yards and watch for the place where it crosses Blodgett Creek. This crossing involves two channels of the creek and can be difficult in high water. Watch for the creek coming from the direction of High Lake. The trail is on the east side of this creek, not on the west as shown on the maps. When I last hiked this trail it was choked with downed trees making it impassible to all but the most stubborn hikers. The Forest Service reports they have no plans to clear it. The lake is about 3.5 miles south and almost 2,000 feet above the junction.

This is a steep, demanding hike, and the trail is extremely rough in places and is hard to find. High Lake is on a shelf high above the floor of Blodgett Canyon. It is fairly large (about one-half mile long) with an irrigation dam at the lake's outlet that detracts from the scenery. The scars from the 1966 rebuilding of the dam are still apparent. The surrounding scenery is well worth the hike. Canyon Peak looms to the southwest, and a sheer rock wall towers above the lake's west side. There is a cabin near the lake.

Now we are back at Blodgett Creek. To reach Blodgett Lake or Blodgett Pass, hike west on the main Blodgett Creek trail, which continues along the north side of the creek. The grade is fairly easy all the way to the junction to Blodgett Pass. The track crosses several large, open meadows, allowing views of the steep canyon walls and of groves of aspen along the canyon's lower flanks. There are several excellent campsites in the four-mile stretch between the High Lake trail junction and the fork to Blodgett Pass. The junction to the pass, about 10.5 miles from the trailhead, is marked by a sign.

Blodgett Lake lies about two miles from the junction. The trail to the lake along Blodgett Creek is poorly maintained and rough in places. It requires a steady if not steep climb. The Lake's alpine environment features towering rock walls which form a large basin at the head of Blodgett Creek. The lake, relatively small but deep, is defaced by an old irrigation dam. Sheer rock walls border it on two sides. The fishing is good, and there are several good campsites near the lake outlet. Blodgett Lake receives only rare visitors.

To reach Blodgett Pass and Big Sand Lake, take the main trail (at the point where the path to Blodgett Lake forks to the southwest). The junction is marked with a rock cairn and sign. From Blodgett Creek, the trail climbs switchbacks created by blasting a narrow ledge that zig-zags up the face of a sheer rock wall. The top of the pass is a steep climb of about 1.5 miles.

From here the trail descends steadily for six miles to Big Sand Lake. The first 3-4 miles of trail from the top of Blodgett Pass to Big Sand Lake is in very poor condition with deeply washed gullies and boggy areas along the trail. This path winds along the bottom of a long canyon with steeply sloping walls. The angle of the canyon walls here appears to be ideal for snow avalanches - there is extensive evidence of numerous large-scale slides. In at least three areas, extensive avalanche activity has created broad bands of flattened trees on the lower flanks of the slope and across the bottom of the canyon, directly across the trail. Although the US Forest Service reports that it clears this trail on an annual basis, persons considering using horses to reach Big Sand Lake should be sure to inquire about the trail's condition.

The trail continues down, following Big Sand Creek. As you descend further into the Big Sand drainage the character of the country changes gradually. From the alpine vegetation at the top of Blodgett Pass, the trail passes through lodgepole pine forest, then enters a valley characterized by thick vegetation. The trail becomes wet and marshy in places as it traverses clearings overgrown with heavy, low brush interspersed with dense forest.

Big Sand Lake lies in a large valley. It is surrounded by heavy forest and marshy meadows. Its shores are composed of white, sandy beaches, and a few sandy fingers extend out into the lake. Big Sand Lake is frequently visited by moose: at times six or eight of the large ungainly creatures can be seen feeding in the lake. They generally browse on the marshy south shore, standing in water with their heads submerged to feed on aquatic vegetation.

For the wildlife photographer, this site presents an exceptional opportunity.

From Big Sand Lake it is possible to complete a point-to-point hike to the Twin Lakes trailhead located fifteen miles south in the Lost Horse area. For details, see "East Fork of Moose Creek to Big Sand Lake." Another option is to hike out to the trailhead at Elk Summit about eight miles to the West on Forest Service Trail #4.

Topographic Maps. Blodgett Mountain; Printz Ridge; Hamilton North; Jeanette Mountain; Saddle Mountain; Tenmile Lake.

21. Blodgett Overlook

The grade is not very steep and the trail is excellent. Scenic views of the Hamilton area below and the Sapphire Mountains to the east are available along the trail. The overlook provides an exceptional vista of the lower end of Blodgett Canyon and is well worth the walk. Use is moderate.

Distance: See Map #4
Overlook...1½

Trailhead Directions. At the traffic light on Highway 93 and Main Street in Hamilton, turn west onto Main Street and drive through town. The road crosses the Bitterroot River on a bridge. At 1.2 miles turn right (north) on Rickets Road and drive one-half mile to Blodgett Camp Road. Turn left (west) and drive 2.5 miles to a road junction. Turn left on the gravel road where the sign designates Canyon Creek and drive two miles to the end. There is ample parking space for about twelve cars.

Trail Description. This is a combined trailhead for both Canyon Creek and Blodgett Overlook. Both share the same trail for the first 20 yards. The trail starts at the west end of the parking lot just beyond the Forest Service information board. About 20 yards beyond the sign the Blodgett Overlook trail forks to the right. This trail climbs gradually, through a series of switchbacks, up the north wall of Canyon Creek. Eventually this trail climbs over the ridge dividing Canyon Creek from Blodgett Canyon, the next drainage to the north.

The path is well constructed offering a smooth, wide trail with a relatively easy grade, winding through widely spaced trees with excellent views of the Hamilton area and the Sapphire Mountains to the east. Several bench rests are located in scenic spots along the trail.

Blodgett Overlook is located on an exposed rocky spire among big ponderosa pines. Splendid views are available of lower Blodgett Canyon and the sheer rock faces of its north wall.

Although reaching the overlook requires a continuous uphill walk, the grade is not very steep because of the moderating effect of the switchbacks. The view at the top is well worth the effort. This trail is not shown on the Selway Bitterroot Wilderness Map.

Topographic Maps. Hamilton North.

22. Canyon Creek

The trail is easy to follow, although in places it is quite steep and is not always in the best condition. Regardless, the views make the effort worthwhile. This out-and-back route features Canyon Falls, as well as three small but pretty lakes. Numerous camping sites are available. Use is moderate.

Distances: See Map #4

Trailhead Directions. At the traffic light on Highway 93 and Main Street in Hamilton, turn west onto Main Street and drive through town. The road crosses the Bitterroot River on a bridge. At 1.2 miles turn right (north) on Rickets Road and drive one-half mile to Blodgett Camp Road. Turn left (west) and drive 2.5 miles on the part-paved, part-gravel road. Then turn left on a gravel road where the sign designates Canyon Creek. Drive two miles to the end. This is the trailhead. The road is excellent and there is ample parking space for about twelve cars.

Trail Description. The trail starts at the west end of the parking area just beyond the Forest Service information board. About 20 yards beyond the trailhead, the "Blodgett Overlook" trail branches to the north. Continue west past this junction. The path is easily followed although it is rough and uneven and is strewn with boulders. Roots creep across the trail, and it is steep in places. It follows the creek and affords a view of the rocky spires that tower above shimmering aspens and fields of boulders. At about four miles the course breaks into the open, then switchbacks steeply up a rocky face of the canyon. This segment offers a splendid view of the falls. Several campsites are available below the falls.

The trail climbs above the falls, then descends into a small meadow to a narrow and shallow pond called East Lake. A stream meanders gently through wide, grassy bends. The path follows this stream to Canyon Lake, elevation 7300 feet. This lovely high lake, contained behind an old irrigation dam constructed of boulders, is cradled in a glacial cirque. It is surrounded by steep walls and (early in the season) by snowfields. There are some excellent campsites both beside the lake and below, along the stream. The remains of old narrow-gauge railroad beds, crumbling concrete, and rusting steel wheels are still visible.

To reach the third lake, follow the creek that flows into the west end of Canyon Lake. This creek's source, Wyant Lake, is one-half mile farther up the canyon. Wyant Lake is a small but lovely jewel which (like Canyon Lake) also is defaced by an irrigation dam. It sits at the head of the deep glacial canyon, close to the bare peaks towering above. Here, from a site of lofty isolation, you can view the town of Hamilton.

Topographic Maps. Ward Mountain; Printz Ridge; Hamilton North.

23. Sawtooth Creek

This trail follows closely along Sawtooth Creek. There are many fishing holes and beaver ponds. The trail is rough and poorly defined beyond its first three miles. It is lightly used and offers good opportunities for solitude. Adventurous hikers may want to try to find Ingomar Lake, a place with no trails but legendary fishing. Use is light.

Distances: See Map #4

End of trail *12*

Ingomar Lake *13½*

Trailhead Directions. From Hamilton, drive 4.1 miles south on Highway 93 to Roaring Lion Road (Mt. Route 531). Turn west on this good road and drive 2.5 miles to the combined Sawtooth-Ward Mountain trailhead. There is lots of space for parking here.

Trail Description. The trailhead is located at the northwest end of the parking area. Go past the gate and follow the old road down to Roaring Lion Creek. Cross the creek here on the foot bridge. The trail contours around the east end of Goat Mountain, which is the ridge separating Roaring Lion Creek from Sawtooth Creek. About one-half mile beyond the creek crossing the trail enters private property. A metal gate allows visitors to pass through this privately owned section. The trail then joins Sawtooth Creek and continues to parallel the stream throughout most of its length.

The first two miles along Sawtooth Creek involve several short, steep climbs. The trail is well defined but rough. Sawtooth Creek is a charming mountain stream, rushing over big rocks and swirling in deep pools. There are several deep fishing holes along this stretch and there is good fishing for small cutthroat trout. About three miles up from the trailhead is the first of the creek crossings. This can be a bad crossing at high water. If you don't want to wade, try hiking upstream. About 200 yards past the crossing is a big log which spans the creek at the foot of a deep pool. I have found this to be a good foot bridge.

Beyond this crossing the trail is more lightly used. The trail is rough in places where it winds through boulder fields. It is also overgrown with brush.

The trail traverses grassy meadows and in places it is hard to find. In addition there are two more creek crossings. Despite the fact that the trail is poorly defined in places, it continues its westward course for about twelve miles (from the trailhead).

A variety of good fishing opportunities are available here with numerous beaver ponds and pools. If you are a hardy hiker and a dedicated fisherman, you may wish to consider trying to find the elusive Ingomar Lake. Many wondrous stories have been told around the campfire about the fishing at Ingomar Lake. While the storytellers describe the beauty of this remote lake and the size of the fish, few people have been there themselves. However, they all claim to know someone who has. It is the legendary "Holy Grail" of the most dedicated Bitterroot fishermen.

The reason why so few people visit Lake Ingomar is it's a tough hike with no trail for the last one and one-half miles and very difficult to find. The map shows it located about ten miles west of the mouth of Sawtooth Canyon. It is perched about 1,200 feet above the valley floor on the south wall. Finding the precise location to leave Sawtooth Creek and start climbing the south wall to Ingomar is essential. If you want to try for Ingomar, be sure to take a compass and map. The "Tenmile Lake Quadrangle" from USGS is a great help. An important landmark to watch for is the creek coming from the south canyon wall. This is the lake outlet stream. The lake is located about one and one-half miles south and 1,200 feet above this stream junction.

Topographic Maps. Tenmile Lake; Ward Mountain; Hamilton South.

24. Roaring Lion Creek

This is a scenic out-and-back hike. It offers good creek access for fishing, and there are several good campsites along the upper portion. The trail's upper segment is poorly defined and difficult to follow. This lightly used trail offers hikers a good chance for isolation among splendid wilderness scenery.

Distances: See Map #4

Trailhead Directions. From Hamilton drive 4.1 miles south on Highway 93 to Roaring Lion Road (Mt. Route 531). Turn right and drive 3.5 miles west to the trailhead at the end of the road. The last mile is very rough. There is a turnaround area and a horse loading ramp.

Trail Description. The trail is marked by a US Forest Service sign, and starts on the south side of the creek. It is level for 200 yards, then climbs steeply for about one-quarter mile. Afterward the pitch is gradual. The canyon is quite narrow at first, but beyond about one-half mile the canyon opens up somewhat and the trail crosses to the creek's north bank. A single log served as a bridge the last time I was here. There is an old cabin site at about one mile.

The south wall of the canyon is timbered, and the north wall is almost sheer rock, with picturesque jagged crags crowning its ridge. The creek, which the trail follows closely, is a rushing mountain stream with deep pools. Access to the creek for fishing requires only a short stroll down to its banks.

For the first three miles the trail offers splendid views of the rugged rock wall on the north side and of the wooded south wall's more gradual slopes. At about 3.5 miles the south wall opens up where a side canyon enters. From here the trail begins to disintegrate and is somewhat rough, with many rocks and roots. The trail winds through several boulder fields. Mountain goats may be seen on the steep slopes above if you watch carefully. There are several nice campsites along the creek. You reach a second creek crossing at 6 miles.

The trail extends about seven miles, climbing on a moderate grade over the last half of its length. Near the end there is a campsite in a cleared area. The trail then crosses the creek and soon vanishes in thick timber, about where the two forks of Roaring Lion Creek meet. The main branch flows down a steep, rocky slope from a small, unnamed lake about two miles west; the other fork flows from the south.

At the head of the canyon, steep, rocky walls form a large basin. This area is rarely visited, and provides hikers an excellent opportunity for solitude. It is a good place to day-hike and to explore the upper Roaring Lion basin - an area with no trails and few people.

Topographic Maps. Ward Mountain; Tenmile Lake; Hamilton South.

25. Ward Mountain

This is a very steep hike throughout. It gains 5,000 feet -- nearly one mile -- in elevation. Because the trail runs for some distance along an exposed south-facing slope, it also can be a very hot trek. This trail frankly is not recommended for persons who are out of shape. Hikers should plan to take their time and should carry plenty of water. This out-and-back hike offers outstanding scenic vistas from the top.

Distances: See Map #4

Burn Area..*2½*

Ward Mountain...*6*

Trailhead Directions. From Hamilton drive 4.1 miles south on Highway 93 to Roaring Lion Road (Mt. Route 531). Turn west on this good road and drive 2.5 miles to the signed trailhead. This is a combined trailhead for Ward Mountain and for Sawtooth Creek. The parking area is on the north side of the road. For the Ward Mountain trail, cross the road to the south side and look for the small sign.

Trail Description. The trail starts climbing almost from its beginning. The first 2.5 miles climb a series of switchbacks with a relatively easy grade. The trail starts climbing through large ponderosa pines. Much of the path is on south facing slopes offering little shade.

About 2.5 miles up the trail you will enter the area burned in the 1994 fires. The trail also starts climbing at a steeper angle. The burned area is interesting to observe. In the spring of 1995 I hiked this trail and noticed that it was stark and naked looking, devoid of the softening effects of grasses, live trees and brush. When I hiked the same trail in late September 1995, I couldn't help but notice the changes. Instead of the blackened clumps of beargrass under foot new growth was evident. Fireweed plants were growing in profusion as were tall grasses and low shrubs.

About 3.5 miles up the trail a short side trail leads to some rocky spires offering a dramatic overlook of the Roaring Lion drainage. Beyond the overlook the trail winds through some unburned green trees and then re-emerges into a burned zone for about one-third mile. Then the burnt areas are left behind.

60

About 1.5 miles from the top, the trail crosses a nice creek, a great relief for those not packing enough water. As the summit grows close, the trees are much more widely spaced offering unobstructed views. When I hiked this in late September, the alpine larch trees offered a glorious golden display of color.

The remains of the lookout tower squat in the lonely splendor of a stark boulder field. All that is left of the lookout is a rock wall foundation and several steel eye bolt anchors embedded in concrete. One concrete pad is inscribed with the legend "JW Brown 1934". Some debris from the lookout still remains scattered about. Rusty nails and shards of glass litter the site.

The site offers magnificent views in all directions. El Capitan Peak to the south seems very close as do the Como Peaks. The trail is in excellent condition. However, the climb is relentless all the way to the top.

Topographic Maps. Ward Mountain; Hamilton South.

26. Coyote Coulee

This trail offers over nine miles of hiking in rolling foothills. The area is forested with widely spaced trees and some very old abandoned apple orchards. The trail consists of two loops joined by a mile long connecting trail. The first loop is 4.4 miles and the second is 2.9 miles and is reached by a .95 mile connecting trail located halfway around the first loop. Hikers may choose only the first loop or to complete both for the full 9.2 miles. The area is inhabited by a considerable variety of wildlife.

This charming double loop trail is the result of a collaborative effort between the Bitterroot Back Country Horsemen Club and The US Forest Service. The Back Country Horsemen developed the route and provided volunteer labor over a five-year period to build the trail. Work on the trail was mostly completed by fall 1997. The trail is dedicated to the late Belle McGregor who helped start this project.

Distances: See Map #8

Note: distances measured in a clockwise direction.

First loop to junction with connecting trail 2.3
Connecting trail 0.95
Second loop 2.9
Connecting trail (again) 0.95
Remainder of first loop 2.1
Total distance..9.2
First loop only...4.4

Trailhead Directions: From Hamilton drive south on Highway 93 for 9.3 miles. Turn right on Lost Horse Road. Drive 2.3 miles west to the end of the pavement, then turn right at the sign for Camas Creek. This is FS Road #496. Drive .2 miles up the road to the "Y"-shaped junction with FS Road #5629. The trailhead is to the right of this junction as you face uphill.

Trail Description: The trail leaves the parking area on an old jeep road, but after a hundred yards or so a junction is reached. Here the hiker must choose a direction to start the first loop. The following trail description is for a clockwise direction on both loops. Watch for the blue diamond shaped trail markers.

Starting on the left fork the trail climbs gradually through a forested area. The widely spaced coniferous trees are interspersed with occasional clusters of aspen. In addition, a great many very old apple trees are scattered for miles throughout these rolling hills. The apple trees are the remnants of the extensive Bitterroot apple orchard developments in the early 1900s.

Moose creek, about .75 miles from the trailhead, is the first creek crossing on this trail. The next crossing, about .25 miles further, is Hayes Creek. Both are small creeks and easily crossed, although in high water you may get wet feet. At 1.5 miles the trail crosses a narrow road. Shortly after this the trail starts to lose elevation and drops into Coyote Coulee. At 2.3 miles is a rock cairn that marks the junction of the connecting trail for the second loop. For those who wish to do the first loop only, turn right at this marker and follow the trail 2.1 miles back to the trailhead.

To reach the second loop follow the connecting trail through the widely scattered trees .95 miles to the start of the second loop. The connecting trail passes the remains of an old homestead. Camas Creek is located about .6 miles beyond the last junction. A good foot log with hand rail spans the creek.

About .3 miles past Camas Creek is the junction for the second loop. Still going in a clockwise direction take the left fork and follow the trail up the ridge. The trail climbs steadily for about .75 miles. After reaching a marshy spot where the trail is raised above the wet bog it begins a gradual descent while following along an old logging road. The trees are widely spaced and provide an open park-like setting. The lower end of this loop trail follows an old rail bed left from the early days when logs were transported from the cutting area on small temporary railways.

After reaching the junction for the beginning of the second loop, follow the connecting trail back to the junction for the first loop. Take the left fork which will allow the completion of the final segment of the first loop. This is a very easy 2.1 mile hike back to the trailhead. The trail climbs briefly for about.25 miles, following an old road up to the top of a low ridge. The trail then crosses the narrow road mentioned earlier and then winds through an area forested by a great many apple trees mixed with aspens. The trail is relatively flat from here back to the trailhead. There is one small creek to cross, this is Hayes Creek.

Maps: Ward Mountain; Hamilton South.

27. Camas Lakes

Kidney Lake and the Camas Lakes all offer fine scenery and good fishing. Countless good campsites abound in the area, both near the lakes and along the trails. By walking a short way past Upper Camas Lake, you can view some lovely alpine scenery. Although this out-and-back trail is poorly defined in some spots, there is little danger of becoming lost. Use is moderate to heavy up to Lower Camas Lake, light beyond Lower Camas Lake.

Distances: See Map #5

Trail junction to Kidney Lake *2¼*
Kidney Lake *3¼*
Burn Area *2¼*
Lower Camas Lake *2½*
Middle Camas Lake *3¼*
Upper Camas Lake *3¾*
Ridge top *4¾*

Trailhead Directions. From Hamilton, drive south on Highway 93 for 9.3 miles. Turn right (west) on Lost Horse Road. Drive 2.3 miles west, then turn right at the Forest Service sign for "Camas

Creek". From here drive 6.1 miles to the signed trailhead. There is parking space for twelve to fifteen cars and a turn around area.

Trail Description. The trail follows an old logging road for the first three-quarters mile. There is a small creek crossing at 300 yards. After the end of the logging road, the trail enters a thickly forested area and climbs more steeply.

Another creek crossing is located about one and three-quarters miles up the trail. For the next one-quarter mile the trail is rough with boulders and roots and it's also muddy in places. Then it climbs steeply for about one-quarter mile and then levels out.

About one-quarter mile below Lower Camas Lake the trail reaches a level stretch. A cairn and a large blaze on a tree both serve as markers for the trail junction to Kidney Lake. There is no sign however, so watch carefully for the junction. To reach Kidney Lake, a rough trail crosses Camas Creek on a single log bridge, then trends generally southeast. The last one-half mile is a steep climb. Kidney Lake, approximately one mile from the trail junction, is encircled by rocky crags. It is a small lake and actually divides into two ponds when the water level drops in late summer. It lies in a high glacial basin with steep walls on three sides and a low glacial moraine at the end. It is a very pretty spot with some excellent campsites. The natural beauty is marred slightly by an old rock and earth irrigation dam. Kidney Lake receives only light use and offers good fishing.

Approaching the first Camas Lake, the trail winds through the scorched trees of a burned area. Lower Camas Lake is a small deep lake bounded by a steep rockslide and rock walls on the north side. Heavy timber surrounds it, and there are several marshy areas. The few campsites are in the timber at the lake's east end. The fishing is good.

Hikers going to the upper lakes can follow either shore around the lake. There is no easy route through the boulders. The trail then follows Camas Creek west, up the slope at the head of the lake. In places the trail is poorly defined, but anyone in doubt can stay on the right side of the creek (going uphill) and just hike in a direction parallel to the creek. Here, the going is quite steep in places, and you may have to scramble up some rock faces on all fours. Some excellent campsites, on flat rocky ledges along here, offer an excellent view of Camas Lake below and the surrounding peaks. This location is much better than sites near the lower lake, because the camper is out of the marshes and trees.

After a walk of about one mile, you will arrive at Middle Camas Lake. This lake is not as closed in by trees as the lower lake, and is much more attractive, with excellent fishing. There are some good campsites at the upper end.

A rough trail runs around the north side of the middle lake. Then a half mile walk upslope along Camas Creek leads to the largest and most attractive of the Camas Lakes. The upper lake has both good fishing and good campsites. The nearby slopes consist of large rock slabs and timber. There are excellent views of the encircling bare rocky peaks, including Ward Mountain to the north.

If you are energetic, the rocky ledges west of the upper lake provide an easy ascent to a scenic treat. In a high alpine fairyland, sinuous streams wind through large, stately fir trees and across broad, open meadows, beyond which gnarled grey trees ascend almost to the windswept spine of the Bitterroots. The surrounding peaks are very close, and snowfields remain on their north-facing slopes, even in mid-August. This is alpine mountain scenery at its very best, and it is well worth the twenty-minute walk above Upper Camas Lake. From the upper lake to the crest of the Bitterroot range is only a forty-five minute walk west. Hikers can simply scramble up the slope on the low ridge to the northwest of Upper Camas Lake. Despite the lack of a well- defined trail, the walking here is easy.

Topographic Maps. Ward Mountain; Hamilton South.

28.East Fork of Moose Creek to Big Sand Lake

This hike may be taken either as an out-and-back hike or as a 35 mile point-to-point hike. The seventeen mile hike to Big Sand Lake follows the trail down the East Fork of Moose Creek and then over a very steep pass between Dead Elk Creek and Little Dead Elk Creek. The East Fork trail is heavily forested and lightly used except in hunting season. The same is true for the two Dead Elk Creek trails. Big Sand Lake is a very attractive place in a heavily forested area. The lake and surrounding area is frequently visited by moose. It is very likely that you will see some of these large ungainly creatures in the lake. Big Sand Lake is a popular destination for stock users and hikers coming in from the Elk Summit area.

For those interested in completing the second leg of a 35 mile point-to-point hike, it is possible to hike east from Big Sand Lake to cross Blodgett Pass and then follow Blodgett Creek downstream to the trailhead eighteen miles away. For details see "Blodgett to Big Sand Lake".

Distances: See Map #4

Moose Lake *4*
Dead Elk Creek Trail Junction *10*
Big Sand Creek Trail Junction *16*
Big Sand Lake *17*
Blodgett Trailhead *35*

Trailhead Directions. From Hamilton drive 9.5 miles south on Highway 93. Turn right on Lost Horse Road. Drive eighteen miles west to the Lost Horse Station, a log cabin identified by a Forest Service sign. From the cabin take the right fork in the road and follow the signs to Twin Lakes, two miles beyond the cabin.

Trail Description. From the trailhead at the north end of the lower lake, cross below the dam of the upper lake and follow the trail to a junction at the upper end of the lake. Twin Lakes are in a lovely high altitude setting and there are very often moose in the lakes. At the junction, follow the trail sign to the East Fork of Moose Creek.

The trail descends steeply for about two miles and then crosses the East Fork at a ford. The area is heavily forested beyond the first half mile. Moose Lake is located about two miles beyond this ford. The lake is not visible from the trail. The area downstream from Moose Lake was extensively burned in the 1988 fires. The lake is located a few hundred yards upstream from the beginning of the burn.

As the trail continues downstream from Moose Lake, the canyon walls close together more tightly. The trail passes through an area where the canyon is narrow and the high walls are heavily forested.

The trail junction to Dead Elk Creek is about ten miles downstream from the Twin Lakes trailhead. The trail junction is signed and is just upstream from the junction of Dead Elk Creek and the East Fork of Moose Creek. The Dead Elk trail is not regularly maintained so you are likely to encounter trees across the trail.

From the East Fork and Dead Elk trail junction, the trail climbs, following Dead Elk Creek upstream for about 1.5 miles. About one-half mile past the junction the trail crosses the creek to its north side. There is a nice waterfall in this area. When the trail leaves Dead Elk Creek, it climbs a very steep switchbacked slope. This is a dry, south facing open slope and it is a steep, hot climb to the top of the ridge. From the saddle at the ridge crest, you can look south into the Dead Elk drainage. The high peak to the southeast is Dead Elk Point.

On the north side of the ridge, about 100 yards over the saddle, there is a campsite with a nice spring close to the trail. From the saddle, the trail descends the steep slope into the Little Dead Elk drainage. After crossing Little Dead Elk Creek, the trail follows the creek north for about two miles through a heavily forested, marshy area to its junction with Big Sand Creek. The trail crosses Big Sand Creek and joins the Big Sand trail (trail 4). There is no sign but a cairn and tree blaze mark the junction. Turn east and follow this excellent trail about one mile to Big Sand Lake.

Big Sand Lake lies in a large valley. It is surrounded by heavy forest and marshy meadows. Its shores are composed of white, sandy beaches, and a few sandy fingers extend out into the lake. Big Sand Lake is frequented by moose. At times, six or eight of the large ungainly creatures can be seen feeding in the lake. They generally browse on the marshy south shore, standing in the water with their heads submerged to feed on aquatic vegetation.

From Big Sand Lake, it is possible to hike east over Blodgett Pass back into Montana and down Blodgett Creek to the Blodgett trailhead near Hamilton. It is about eighteen miles to the Blodgett trailhead. For details see "Blodgett Canyon to Big Sand Lake".

Topographic Maps. Jeanette Mountain; Saddle Mountain; Tenmile Lake.

29. Wahoo Pass to Bear Creek Loop

This is a 36 mile scenic loop trail starting at Twin Lakes and going west over Wahoo Pass. The area around Wahoo Pass is especially nice alpine terrain offering splendid views of the high country. The trek continues down Wahoo Creek to a trail junction with the

Pettibone Ridge trail. A side trip to lovely Indian Lake may also be included. The hike continues along Pettibone Ridge to the southwest and then descends a very steep ridge to join the Bear Creek trail.

A charming hike up Bear Creek through some enchanted cedar groves leads to the east, and Bear Creek Pass. From Bear Creek Pass, it is about three miles over a forest service road to the Twin Lakes trailhead.

Although this is not technically a true loop hike, it seems unlikely that a hiker willing to traverse the 33 miles of rough trail will quibble over hiking three miles on a remote road to complete the loop.

Distances (from Twin Lakes trailhead): See Map #7
Pettibone Ridge Indian Lake Trail Junction..........11
Indian Lake 13½
Bear Creek Trail Junction 20
Bear Creek Pass...33
Twin Lakes Trailhead 36

Trailhead Directions. From Hamilton drive 9.5 miles south on Highway 93. Turn right on Lost Horse Road. Drive eighteen miles west to the Lost Horse Station, a log cabin identified by a Forest Service sign. From the cabin take the right fork in the road and follow the signs to Twin Lakes two miles beyond the cabin. Continue along the road on the west side of the Lower Twin Lake to the trailhead located just before the dam on the upper Twin Lake.

Trail Description. The trail crosses below the dam separating the upper lake from the lower lake. The lakes are in a lovely high altitude setting. It is quite common to see moose in the lakes. After crossing the dam, the trail follows the east shore of the upper lake. Just past the upper end of the lake, is the signed trail junction for

70

East Fork Moose Creek and Wahoo Pass trails. The left fork leading uphill and to the west is the Wahoo Pass trail.

The trail winds past a small lake and climbs a steep switchbacked slope offering splendid views of the lakes below. From the top of Wahoo Pass at about 7,000 feet elevation, there is an excellent view down Wahoo Canyon to the west and of the many bare granite peaks. The trail then begins a steep descent. The upper end of the Wahoo Pass trail is switchbacked and there are a number of small creeks crossing the trail. The trail is mostly in open country offering continuous views of the canyon.

The trail continues to follow Wahoo Creek for about five miles, dropping about 1,800 feet until it crosses Big Creek. It then leaves Wahoo Creek behind and begins to climb a steep ridge. After climbing about 1,600 feet in 2.5 miles, it heads in a southwesterly direction along a hillside. The trail reaches the Indian Lake-Pettibone Ridge junction about eleven miles from the trailhead. The right fork at this junction is Trail 430 which leads to Indian Lake, a most excellent place to visit.

Indian Lake is about 2.5 miles west of the trail junction. There is a sign here. The trail from the junction loses about 600 feet of elevation in about two miles. After crossing Pettibone Creek, it climbs very gradually to Indian Lake. The lake is in a lovely high altitude setting. It is about one-half mile long and its elevation is 6,130 feet. There are wooded hills around the south and northwest sides of the lake. The northeast end has some big open meadows. There is an outfitter camp located at the northeast end of the lake. On a personal note, I would be interested in hearing from readers who have fished here.

A trail leading west from Indian Lake leads to Horsefly Meadows, located about two miles west of the lake. These huge open grassy meadows are a great place to see wildlife. The Forest Service trail crew told me they did not maintain the trail to the west beyond Horsefly Meadows.

After a side trip to the Indian Lake area, we are now back at the trail junction about 2.5 miles east of Indian Lake. The trail leading to the southwest is the Pettibone Ridge trail, also known as trail 634. From the junction the trail climbs for about one-half mile and then drops down to cross a creek. It then starts climbing again for about 2.5 miles and then starts loosing altitude rapidly. Portions of this trail traverse an area that was burned in the 1988 fires. Consequently, there may be blowdown trees across the trail. In addition, this trail is not maintained every year but is on a three-year rotation for maintenance.

About six miles southwest of the Indian Lake Trail junction, there is a nice campsite with a good spring located at a saddle, just north of the junction of trail 634 and 642.

Trail 642 is the trail leading southeast down the ridge to join the Bear Creek Trail. It is very steep, and loses about 3,000 feet of elevation in about two miles. It is also a rough trail that is not regularly maintained.

From the junction with Bear Creek, it is about thirteen miles to the trailhead at Bear Creek Pass. The trail climbs very gradually following the north side of Bear Creek. The trail passes through an area forested with huge cedar trees. The cedar groves, which continue for the next seven miles, are very different from the pine forest at higher elevations. Here the trees are widely spaced and the area below the trees is shaded and cool. There is no underbrush. Ferns grow beneath the huge trees and it is very quiet. It is a very different experience to hike through the miles of cedar groves.

About six miles below Bear Creek Pass, the trail begins to climb more steeply. The very wide trail climbs a series of gradual switchbacks that appear to have been constructed as a wagon road. The trail climbs about 1,800 feet over the next six miles to the trailhead at Bear Creek Pass. From here it is about three miles over the gravel road to the Twin Lakes trailhead where the hike started.

Topographic Maps. Hunter Peak; Twin Butte; Saddle Mountain; Dog Creek.

30. Bailey Lake

This short walk is a good beginner's trail. It is just right for anyone who wants only to spend an afternoon in the woods at a pretty lake. The trail is just 1.5 miles long, and the hiking is quite enjoyable. Use is light.

Distances: See Map #5
Bailey Lake..1½

Trailhead Directions. From Hamilton, drive 9.5 miles south on Highway 93. Then turn right (west) on Lost Horse Road. Drive 18.2 miles to the Lost Horse Guard Station. The Bailey Lake trailhead is about 100 yards past the guard station. The trailhead is on the right and is signed. There is no designated parking area but there is adequate room to pull off the road.

Trail Description. This is an easy hike to a small mountain lake. It climbs gradually but steadily to Bailey Lake, gaining perhaps 700 feet elevation in about 1.5 miles. Bailey Lake is an attractive lake at the head of one of the branches of Lost Horse Creek. It is small - no more than one-quarter mile in length and quite shallow. This area was burned in 1988. The trail is cluttered with fallen trees as it switchbacks up the slope. In places you have to watch carefully for rock cairns to stay on the trail.

Bailey Lake is used primarily by day hikers and fishermen and is a bit too close to the trailhead for good camping. Yet it is a lovely spot for folks who want only to walk a short distance, and for novice campers who want to give hiking and camping a try. It has fair fishing.

Topographic Maps. Tenmile Lake; Saddle Mountain.

31. Fish Lake

This is a lovely place to hike. The trail passes above Lower Bear Lake before climbing over a ridge to Fish Lake. There are often moose in Lower Bear Lake. The trail to Fish Lake switchbacks down to the lake about 500 feet below the pass. The lake is in a lovely setting framed by outstanding scenic peaks to the south. The lake is a high altitude jewel, offering good campsites and fishing opportunities. Use is moderate.

Distances: See Map #5
Lower Bear Lake..1
Trail Junction to Upper Bear Lake.................1½
Upper Bear Lake..1¾
Fish Lake...4

Trailhead Directions. From Hamilton, drive 9.5 miles south on Highway 93, then turn right on Lost Horse Road. Drive 18.2 miles west to the Lost Horse Station, a log cabin identified by a US Forest Service sign. At the cabin, take the left fork and follow the sign pointing to Bear Creek Pass. Drive 1.2 miles to the Forest

Service campground, then watch for the trailhead signs for Fish Lake and Bear Lake. The trailhead is on the south edge of the campground.

Trail Description. Follow the trail from the southwest corner of the campground. The trail winds through trees and rocks climbing gradually. About one mile from the trailhead, the trail climbs a steep ridge and then crosses the south facing slope above Lower Bear Lake. The lake lies in a very pretty setting below. There is a large, open meadow with a shallow, marshy lake on the east end. The entire setting is framed by high peaks. Moose are often seen in the lake. The trail continues across the slope and then descends into a wooded draw where it climbs again. About one-half mile above Lower Bear Lake is a trail junction. The left fork leads up a steep switchbacked trail to Fish Lake. The right fork leads to Upper Bear Lake, only one-quarter mile from the junction. Upper Bear Lake is a lovely place, but its charm is flawed somewhat by a large old unused irrigation dam.

The trail to Fish Lake switchbacks up a steep ridge from the trail junction. From the pass above, there is a sensational view of Upper Bear Lake on one side and Fish Lake on the other. Fish Lake is a long, deep body with high peaks and rock faces on thee sides. It is among the more spectacular lakes in the high Bitterroots. It nestles at the head of a high mountain canyon. There is an excellent campsite at the pass, with water less than a quarter of a mile down the trail towards Fish Lake. From here the trail switchbacks down the ridge towards the lake, winding through lots of huckleberry bushes. Watch for berries in season, and for moose here as well. There are some excellent campsites close to the lower end of the lake and below its outlet. There is good fishing in the lake and in the creek below the lake.

The map shows a trail following the South Fork of Lost Horse Creek to its junction with Lost Horse Creek. Unfortunately this trail is no longer maintained. The area was burned in the 1988 fires and the Forest Service abandoned this trail. I have tried to hike this area and found the many fallen trees to be a considerable obstacle. I don't recommend this trail!

Topographic Maps. El Capitan; Como Peak; Saddle Mountain.

32. Coquina Lake

This attractive high mountain lake offers good fishing, fine mountain scenery, and the opportunity to see a moose or two. The hike is relatively easy, gaining only 800 feet in 2.8 miles. Refer to Map # 5.

Distance: 2.8.

Trailhead Directions. From Hamilton take US-93 south for 9.5 miles and turn right on the Lost Horse Road. Drive 18 miles up this scenic mountain canyon to the Lost Horse Guard Station. At the cabin, take the left fork and follow the sign for Bear Creek Pass. Drive 1.2 miles to the campground. There is room for dozens of vehicles here. There are campground facilities near the trailhead. A stock ramp and hitch rails are available.

Trail Description. The trailhead is on the southern edge of the campground. The trail winds through trees and rocks climbing gradually. At one mile it ascends a steep ridge and then contours around the end of the ridge to reach the south-facing slope above Lower Bear Lake. Below is a large, open meadow with a shallow, marshy lake on the east end. The setting is framed by high peaks. Moose are often seen in the lake. The trail contours across the slope and then descends into a wooded draw where it climbs again. You reach a trail junction one half mile above Lower Bear Lake. Take the right fork to Upper Bear Lake. The trail crosses Bear Creek and climbs to an old unused irrigation dam. A shallow pond is all that remains of Upper Bear Lake. The trail climbs in a southwesterly direction past the dam. Although it is not shown on the Forest Service map, the tread is clearly defined. There are a few bare rock segments where you should watch for rock cairns marking the route. One mile past Upper Bear Lake the route levels out in a forested area. From here there is an obvious path down the slope to reach Coquina Lake. This is an attractive, small, high mountain lake partially surrounded by granite peaks. The fishing can be quite good. A variety of campsites are available. This would make an easy backpack for a novice.

Map: USGS El Capitan.

33. Bear Creek Pass to Moose Creek to Twin Lakes Loop

This is a 75 mile loop hike. It starts at Bear Creek Pass on the Montana-Idaho border and follows Bear Creek downstream to its junction with the Selway River 23 miles to the west. It then follows the Selway River trail thirteen miles north to the Moose Creek Ranger Station. From there the route follows Moose Creek and then the East Fork of Moose Creek to the Twin Lakes Trailhead and back to Bear Creek Pass.

The trail down Bear Creek is a delightful trek, following along the north side of the creek. The trail is very good and the descent is quite gradual. There are some splendid viewpoints along the trail where the entire upper end of Bear Creek Canyon may be seen.

As the trail loses altitude descending towards the Selway River, the vegetation changes. The lower altitude climate zones are characterized by different trees and plants. The trail winds through a splendid grove of huge cedar trees about seven miles below the trailhead. Hiking through the miles of cedar groves is an especially enjoyable experience.

After the Bear Creek junction at the Selway River, the trail follows the Selway downstream to the Moose Creek Ranger Station. The hike along the river trail is different and rewarding. The river is rich in interesting sights. Waterfowl and big game animals are attracted to the river. The rapids and deep pools are impressive. There are a few camping areas with sandy beaches along the river's edge. Moose Creek Ranger Station provides a jolt of civilization. There is a public airstrip with an enormous runway here. There is also a cluster of log buildings, complete with lots of livestock and people.

To complete the 75 mile loop, the trail follows Moose Creek and then the East Fork of Moose Creek upstream. The Moose Creek hike is also an enjoyable experience. There is another fantastic cedar grove along this trail. This is also a well maintained mainline trail that is easy to follow. Much of the trail is in heavily forested areas contrasting with the hike along the river. The East Fork trail leads to the Twin Lakes trailhead and from there it's a three mile hike over the remote forest service road to the trailhead at Bear Creek Pass where the hike began.

Distances (from Bear Creek Pass): See Map #7
Cub Creek junction *18*
Selway River...*23*
Moose Creek Ranger Station *36*

78

Trailhead Directions. From Hamilton, drive 9.5 miles south on Highway 93. Then turn right on Lost Horse Road. Drive 18.2 miles west to the Lost Horse Station, a log cabin identified by a US Forest Service sign. At the cabin, take the left fork and follow the road to the Bear Creek trailhead. The parking area is just past the trailhead.

Trail Description. The Bear Creek Trail is signed. Hike west on this wide well maintained trail, heading downhill. About 2.5 miles down the trail, there is an especially nice overlook point on a flat bench that provides a good view of upper Bear Creek Canyon. The surrounding granite peaks and the towering canyon's walls provide spectacular scenery.

Beyond the flat bench the trail begins a long and very gradual switchbacked descent. The grade on the switchbacks is very easy and the switchbacks provide numerous overlooks, with wonderful views. Much of the south facing slope above the trail has been burned. The fires burned in a mosaic pattern, leaving islands of charred trees intermingled with stands of green.

The trail is different because it is so wide. It is apparent that the trail was constructed by making a very deep cut into the side of the hill. I think heavy equipment was used in its original construction. Possibly the trail was constructed as a wagon road.

About six miles below the trailhead, the trail enters an area where huge cedar trees predominate. The trail under the cedar trees is carpeted with needles, providing a soft and quiet passage. The trees are widely spaced and the parklike area beneath the shady canopy is free of underbrush. Ferns and other shade loving plants grow here. It's a cool oasis on a hot August day. It's a majestic place, very quiet and restful. Some of the trees are gigantic. The cedars continue for about six miles downstream.

The trail crosses several side creeks and there are some good campsites along the trail and close to the creek. The trail continues along the north side of Bear Creek for the entire distance to the Selway River.

There are some good campsites at the junction with the Selway River. The trail leading upstream goes to the Paradise trailhead, about 18 miles south on the river trail. The downstream trail heading north, follows the river along its east bank to the Moose Creek Ranger Station.

The river trail can be a demanding hike depending on the season. You should stay alert for rattlesnakes. The trail is well maintained and there are bridges crossing the side creeks. There are several camping areas next to the river.

The wild and scenic Selway River is a great treat for kayakers and rafters. The number of river users is restricted by a permit system so it is unlikely you will see many people here. The river's rapids and deep pools are charming. The river trail can get very hot in late summer. There is little shade especially in the afternoon. It's best to get an early start for this stretch. As the trail leads north the route climbs high above the river to avoid the steep cliffs. This is a rugged segment to hike in summer. I prefer to hike this area in October or early May.

The Moose Creek Ranger Station, located about thirteen miles north of the Bear Creek-Selway junction, is a real surprise. This ranger station, deep inside the Selway-Bitterroot Wilderness, includes a public airstrip with an enormous runway. The airfield is about three-quarters of a mile long. It is used by the Forest Service and the general public and is especially busy during hunting season. For those so inclined, it is possible to arrange for a charter aircraft to meet you here to fly out or to resupply.

The ranger station is located on the north end of the runway. This collection of log structures, horse corrals and a few tents, looks like the set for a western movie. In the summer, there are usually several people here and lots of horses and mules. I find it a bit of a shock after several days on the trail.

The trail to Twin Lakes trailhead follows Moose Creek upstream from the ranger station. About one-half mile north of the ranger station is a large parcel of private property on the west bank of Moose Creek. This private inholding is known as the Freeman Place. You can see some buildings from the trail. About one mile north of the station, the trail winds through a very large open meadow. About four miles north of the station, the trail crosses the East Fork of Moose Creek on a good bridge. There is a three-way signed trail junction just north of the bridge. Trail 421 is the main East Fork trail and will lead all the way to the Twin Lakes trailhead. Take the right fork at the junction and follow the East Fork upstream. This is an excellent trail, well maintained and very pleasant. It climbs very gradually and the hiking is easy. About eight miles upstream of the junction, the trail reaches an area known as the Elbow Bend. Here the East Fork changes its heading from east to north.

As the East Fork swings north, the character of the forest changes as well. For the next six miles the trail winds through another magnificent cedar forest.

The trail then begins to climb a little more steeply as it enters a more confined canyon. The trail crosses the East Fork about eleven miles east of the Elbow Bend and there are several more crossings before reaching the trailhead. I had no difficulty with any of the creek crossings in August.

When you reach the sign for the Dead Elk Creek trail junction, you are only about ten miles from the Twin Lakes trailhead. From here the trail follows a deep, narrow canyon surrounded by high forested walls. The trail crosses the East Fork again about 3.5 miles upstream from the Dead Elk junction. After the creek crossing the trail climbs more steeply. About two miles further upstream is Moose Lake. It is a small, marshy lake often visited by (you guessed it) moose! Moose Lake is not visible from the trail.

From Moose Lake, the East Fork trail continues south, climbing along the creek for another four miles. After crossing the East Fork for the last time, the trail climbs steeply for its last two miles to the trail junction at the north end of Twin Lakes. Follow the trail around Twin Lakes and then down the road another three miles to the trailhead at Bear Creek Pass where the hike started.

Topographic Maps. Shissler Peak; Freeman Peak; Wahoo Peak; Hunter Peak; Twin Butte; Dog Creek; Moose Ridge; Cedar Ridge; Tenmile Lake; Saddle Mountain.

34. Spruce Creek to Bear Creek Loop

This is a 40 mile loop hike through some extremely remote, very rough country. The loop trail starts at Bear Creek Pass which is located on the Idaho-Montana border. The trail crosses a high mountain pass and leads past Spruce Lake, a remote high mountain lake which is seldom visited. The Spruce Creek trail then continues downhill to join Paradise Creek, which in turn continues a downhill and westward trend to a junction with Bear Creek. The Spruce Creek-Paradise Creek area is rarely visited by people except during the hunting season. The area is well populated with charismatic megafauna.

The loop trail from Spruce Creek joins the Bear Creek trail about eighteen miles west of Bear Creek Pass and it follows Bear Creek up the canyon to the trailhead where the hike started. The hike along Bear Creek is especially appealing because the trail winds through about six miles of cedar groves. These gigantic cedar trees provide a cool, shaded forest clear of underbrush. It's a magic place to visit. Use is light.

Distances (from Bear Creek Pass trailhead): See Map #7
   Spruce Lake..6½
   Junction with Bear Creek Trail........................22
   Bear Creek Pass...40

Trailhead Directions. From Hamilton, drive 9.5 miles south on Highway 93, then turn right on Lost Horse Road. Drive 18.2 miles west to the Lost Horse Station, a log cabin identified by a US Forest Service sign. At the cabin, take the left fork and follow the sign to Bear Creek Pass. Drive 1.2 miles to the Forest Service campground. The parking area is just past the sign for Bear Creek trail.

Trail Description. The Bear Creek trailhead is signed. Hike west on this trail for one-quarter mile to the Spruce Creek trail. The trail sign is located just past the Selway-Bitterroot Wilderness sign. The trail winds through a wet, marshy area for about one-quarter mile, then it starts climbing in steep switchbacks. Granite peaks loom to both the south and north. There are many wet and muddy places along this trail. The trail is not only steep and muddy, but it's very rough with rocks and roots underfoot. It climbs up a steep ridge, passing an unnamed small lake to the west and then passes a boulder field. There are dramatic views of surrounding peaks. A pass leading to Spruce Lake is reached at about 5 miles. There is a very attractive place to camp at the top of the pass (about 7,200 feet) if you are willing to carry water from the last creek about one-quarter mile back. About 100 feet below the pass there is an exceptional view of Spruce Lake.

The descent to Spruce Lake is very steep and the switchbacked trail is rough. Spruce Lake is about 1.5 miles below the pass at 6,645 feet elevation. The lake is a deep green tarn nestled at the base of a bare, rocky cliff at its upper end. The lake is about one-third mile long with trees crowding close to its south and north shores. There is a campsite at the lower end of the lake next to the trail.

The trail crosses Spruce Creek just below the lake and then follows the creek closely downstream. The trail heads south for about one mile below Spruce Lake then turns west towards its junction with Bear Creek. The trail follows a much more gradual descent after leaving the lake.

About six miles past Spruce Lake, Spruce Creek joins Paradise Creek and its name changes to Paradise Creek. There is an old trail junction here. This side trail coming from the east along Paradise Creek is the remnant of an old trail that formerly connected the Paradise Creek trail with the Rock Creek trail on the Montana side of the Bitterroots. However, if you follow the old Paradise Creek trail back upstream, you will find it ends in a maze of blowdown trees about one mile east of the junction.

The Paradise Creek trail going west from the Spruce Creek-Paradise Creek junction continues to follow closely along the north bank of the creek. The area is heavily forested and the canyon is fairly narrow. About three miles below the junction, the canyon grows wider and for another three miles there are some nice flat places for campsites. About six miles past the junction, the canyon squeezes together and becomes very narrow. The trail begins to drop more steeply as well.

About 1.5 miles before the junction with Bear Creek, Paradise Creek joins another creek, thereby becoming Cub Creek. There is also a trail junction here. The Cub Creek trail follows Cub Creek to the south and eventually joins Brushy Fork Creek. The Spruce

Creek-Paradise Creek-Cub Creek trail then turns northwest and joins Bear Creek about 1.5 miles downstream.

Although some of the maps show a bridge crossing Bear Creek at this junction, there is no bridge! There is a big log jam on Bear Creek that allows a dry crossing. This can be a dangerous crossing depending on the season. If the log jam is no longer in place when you get there, my advice is to be very cautious.

The Bear Creek trail follows along the north side of Bear Creek for eighteen miles going east to Bear Creek Pass. The total elevation gain from this junction to the Bear Creek trailhead is about 3,200 feet. This is a good trail throughout that distance and the elevation gain is gradual for most of the distance. Bear Creek Canyon is relatively wide and there are many good places to camp throughout much of the hike out.

About four miles above the Cub Creek junction, the trail enters an area forested with huge cedar trees. The cedar groves are different from the pine, spruce and fir forests. The trees are widely spaced and the area below the trees is shaded and cool and clear of brush and small trees. Ferns grow beneath the huge trees and it's cool and quiet. It is a very impressive experience to hike through the next six or seven miles of cedar groves.

About six miles below the Bear Creek Pass trailhead, the trail begins to climb more steeply. The very wide trail climbs a series of gradual switchbacks that appear to have been constructed as a wagon road. The trail climbs about 1,800 feet over the next six miles returning to the trailhead at Bear Creek Pass.

Topographic Maps. Hunter Peak; Twin Butte.

35. Lake Como Loop

This is an easy, very picturesque hike, ideal as a preseason hike for out-of-shape individuals. It is a very pleasant hike at any time, and during the winter the area can be good for skiing or snowshoeing. The setting of the lake is classic with the Como Peaks in the background towering over the lake below. The large earth-filled dam and the excessive late-season drawdown on the lake for irrigation purposes tend to detract from the natural beauty. The well marked sandy swimming beach and developed picnic area provides hikers a good opportunity to cool off after their walk. Use is heavy.

Distances (in counter-clockwise direction): See Map #5
Rock Creek Bridge *3*
Complete lake loop ....*7 ½*

Trailhead Directions. From Hamilton, drive twelve miles south on Highway 93 to the Lake Como Road. Turn right and drive west three miles to the road junction. Turn right at the swimming beach sign and follow the signs. Drive .6 mile past the beach to the north shore trailhead, which is located in the campground.

The north shore trail may be used only by hikers and bicycles; it is closed to horses and motorcycles. The other trailhead is at the southeast end of the lake. This course follows the south shore of the lake, and may be used by horses. There are full facilities at both trailheads. Both have ample parking areas. In addition, the south shore trailhead has a horse loading area and a boat ramp. To reach the south trailhead just follow the paved road below the dam to the signed "Rock Creek Trailhead".

Trail Description. A very good well-marked, and well maintained trail starts west of the north shore campground and parallels the north shore of Lake Como. The first quarter mile is paved for handicapped use. This trail provides the hiker an easy path with few changes in elevation. It offers magnificent views of the lake and of the Como peaks, and there are numerous wildflowers in the area. The trail crosses several small creeks and provides good access to the lake for fishing at a variety of locations. The distance from the trailhead to the west end of the lake, where Rock Creek flows in, is about three miles. Rock Creek is a fair-size stream. The forest on the west end of Lake Como was burned in 1988. The forest's recovery is interesting to observe.

At the west end the trail joins the Rock Creek trail, and a bridge crosses the creek. Take the left fork across the bridge to complete the lake loop to the south shore trailhead. The south shore trail is another excellent, well-used track. It is used heavily by horse packers. The end of the trail is reached at the southeast corner of the lake. If you left a car at the north shore campground, you may just walk across the top of the large earth dam to the swimming beach and follow the road to the campground and trailhead.

Topographic Maps. Como Peaks; Darby.

36. Rock Creek to Elk Lake and Bell Lake

Many portions of this hike offer spectacular scenery. The Rock Creek trail offers excellent trailside fishing opportunities in several deep pools along the path to Elk Lake and to Bell Lake across the Montana-Idaho divide. Side trails are available leading to Capitan Lake, Mile Post Lake, and the two Grizzly Lakes. Excellent fishing may be found at several of these high lakes as well as spectacular scenery. Use is heavy around Lake Como, light to Elk Lake and beyond.

Distances (from north shore trailhead): See Map #5

Elk Lake *12*
Capitan Lake *13*
Bell Lake *14½*
Mile Post Lake *15*
Little Grizzly Lake *15¼*
Big Grizzly Lake *15½*

Trailhead Directions. From Hamilton, drive twelve miles south on Highway 93 to the Lake Como Road. Follow the signs to Lake Como. At the road junction turn right and follow the signs for the swimming area on the north side of the lake. Drive past the beach to the campground and the trailhead west of the beach. The first one-quarter mile of this National Recreation Trail is paved for handicapped access.

Trail Description. The trail to Rock Creek follows the north shore of Lake Como. It is a delightful walk with lovely views of the shining water and the high Como peaks. The junction with the south side trail is just past the end of the lake.

The right fork at this junction leads upstream and west to Elk Lake. The trail, deep in a steeply walled, heavily forested canyon, follows the north side of Rock Creek all the way to Elk Lake. Looming peaks to the north, south, and west provide spectacular scenery. The trail is good but there are many wet and muddy places. The climb is quite gradual: in the nine-mile distance between Como and Elk Lake the elevation gain is only about 1,400 feet. There are several attractive cascades in the creek where the rushing stream spills over rocks in a gush of swirling water and foam. There are several very large pools that offer good fishing. There are also several campsites along the trail.

At about ten miles from the trailhead an unmarked trail branches to the south. This trail, not shown on the maps, crosses Rock Creek and follows Capitan Creek. The trail continues for about three miles leading to Lake Capitan located west of El Capitan Peak. This trail is not maintained by the Forest Service.

Elk Lake is about one-half mile long and one-quarter mile wide and sits in a deep, glaciated canyon. Steep forested walls rise from its rocky south shore to high bare ridges. Barren rocky peaks and ridges loom to the west and south. Some good campsites are found along the north shore, which has been known to provide some excellent fishing. The upper end of the lake is very shallow. The campsites at Elk Lake are badly overused. I would not recommend camping there.

Bell Lake lies about 2.5 miles west. The trail leads around the north shore of Elk Lake and follows the north side of Rock Creek. It starts to climb steeply about one mile above Elk Lake, and gains about 1,000 feet in elevation in the next 1.5 miles. The trail between Elk Lake and Bell Lake differs from the area below Elk Lake. The trail winds through hillside meadows with widely spaced trees, low shrubs and open grassy areas in varying shades of green bordered by rock ridges. There are several excellent campsites located along this stretch of trail. Personally I preferred camping along the edge of one of these meadows than along the lake shore. This is also a much better area for horse camps.

At the top of the pass a blazed tree marks a trail junction and also the Montana-Idaho border. The Bell Lake trail continues west around the north shore of Bell Lake. The trail branching to the south is not shown on the maps. It leads to Mile Post Lake and to the Grizzly Lakes.

Bell Lake lies only a few hundred yards west of the top of the pass. There is a nice campsite just past the trail junction. The lake looks very deep and spruce trees crowd its shores. There is also a good campsite on the north shore about half way around the lake.

The maps indicate that trail No. 522 continues past Bell Lake west to the junction with Paradise Creek. Be advised that this trail no longer exists! The trail has been abandoned for many years and is all but impassable.

The Mile Post Lake trail branches south from the trail junction at the top of the pass. This is an easy to follow trail. It is about one-half mile to Mile Post Lake. The trail continues about one-half mile to Little Grizzly Lake and then another quarter-mile to Big Grizzly Lake. These three high alpine lakes are in a basin surrounded on three sides by towering rock walls. A lovely place to visit, well worth the effort.

Topographic Maps. Como Peaks; El Capitan.

37. Little Rock Creek Lake

This out-and-back course is quite steep and has a rough trail. The lake itself is attractive, the surrounding peaks are spectacular, and some good campsites can be found in the area. There are some very pretty small lakes above Little Rock Creek Lake. Use is moderate. See Map #5

Distance:
Little Rock Creek Lake.....................5

Trailhead Directions. From Hamilton, drive twelve miles south on Highway 93. Turn west (right) on Lake Como Road. Drive 2.9

miles to the road junction just below Lake Como. Turn left, following the sign to Little Rock Creek trail, and go 3.8 miles (from the junction) to a second sign for the Little Rock Creek trail. Drive .2 mile to the trailhead. The road is good for the entire distance. The trailhead is signed and the road is closed beyond this point by a locked gate.

Trail Directions. The trail starts above Lake Como, high on a ridge offering spectacular views of the lake. The trail begins in an area burned in the 1988 fires. It climbs for a short distance, then drops steeply along an open slope dotted with large ponderosa pines. From here there is a lovely view of the lake and the high peaks beyond.

The trail continues to descend, meeting the creek at the mouth of the canyon where it leaves the burned area behind. Then it starts climbing again, following Little Rock Creek through the narrow, steep canyon. Sheer rock cliffs tower above, and a view appears of jagged, rocky peaks, their flanks snow-covered even in mid-August. There is a wilderness-area sign just after entering the canyon. From here the trail is only occasionally maintained and becomes very rough: a lot of rocks, roots, and downed trees make for rough travel. It is a poor trail for horses and slow going for the hiker. For about 2.5 miles the course is so overgrown it appears jungle-like. Then it starts climbing steeply to open, rocky slopes. There are several campsites in these open areas; one is right on the trail. The trail continues to the lake through heavy brush and across occasional open rock faces.

The lake lies in a glacial cirque at 6,545 feet elevation. It has high, steep walls on the north side and boulders and heavy forest on the south. It also has good fishing. At its outlet the lake has an irrigation dam, a water control gate, and an old rock wall five or six feet high. The small, old dam is unobtrusive. Few traces of construction remain, and the water gate control mechanism appears broken and unused.

91

Several campsites can be found at the lower end of the lake. There are waterfalls just below the lake. This area provides good access for those interested in climbing El Capitan which is located less than three miles to the southwest. There are three lakes about two miles southwest just at the base of El Capitan. Located in a spectacular setting, they are well worth the extra hike. Just follow the creek upstream. It's about a 500 foot climb to the lowest of the three.

Topographic Maps. Darby; Como Peaks.

38. Tin Cup to Boulder

Tin Cup Creek trail offers a good variety of mountain scenery and easy hiking conditions. The first three miles climb at a very easy grade but the trail is enclosed in heavy forest. Beyond the first creek crossing, the trail climbs at a slightly steeper angle. Here the canyon opens widely providing exceptional views of the steep walled spectacular canyon. About four miles up the trail is a lovely waterfall and a very pleasant clearing. For those willing to hike a bit further, Tin Cup Lake offers good fishing and spectacular scenery. For the long distance hiker, here is an opportunity to do an extended point-to-point hike of over 50 miles. A trek over the Bitterroot divide furnishes hikers sweeping vistas and leads to the picturesque Triple Lakes. Beyond the lakes you can trek to Coopers Flat along White Cap Creek and then turning east will ascend Canyon Creek. A second crossing of the Bitterroot-Selway divide leads to Boulder Lake and to the Boulder Creek trailhead, 51 miles away. Use is moderate to Tin Cup Lake and light beyond.

Distances (from Tin Cup trailhead): See Map #6

Trailhead Directions. From the Darby Post Office, drive one-quarter mile south on Highway 93 and turn west on Tin Cup Road. Follow the signed road west. About 100 yards beyond the end of the pavement, Tin Cup Road takes a sharp left turn and climbs a hill. It is a 3.5 mile drive from Highway 93 to the trailhead. When you reach the junction with road 639B, turn left and cross the bridge to the trailhead. There is a large parking area. For Boulder Creek Trailhead directions, see Boulder Creek.

Trail Description. The trail starts on the west side of the road and follows the south side of Tin Cup Creek for the first three miles. The trail is well maintained and relatively easy. For the first three miles, the grade is very gradual. The trail is mostly in heavy forest. At about 1.5 miles the trail becomes noticeably wider, almost like a road. The trail follows an old bulldozer road for most of the distance to Tin Cup Lake. The bulldozer road was built in order to move heavy equipment to Tin Cup Lake for the purpose of building and maintaining an irrigation dam.

At three miles, the trail crosses to the north side of the creek. There is a single log that serves as a scary foot bridge just above the horse crossing. After crossing to the creek's north side, the trail begins to climb a little more steeply. The canyon begins to open up at this point and is no longer enclosed by heavy forest. The trees are more widely spaced and there are numerous clearings along the creek. About one mile past the crossing is a lovely cascade with a very pleasant clearing next to the creek, a delightful place for a picnic. As the trail climbs, the canyon walls spread farther apart offering lovely views of the towering ridge tops on both sides of the canyon, while the creek rushes below. This is an especially attractive section of the canyon.

At about six miles, the trail crosses back to the south side of the creek. There is a convenient single log foot bridge available here. The trail continues to climb gradually, but steadily, along this wide part of the canyon. There is good access to the creek offering tempting fishing opportunities throughout most of its length. There is an exceptionally nice clearing next to the creek about one mile past the second crossing. Here the creek is squeezed tightly between narrow rock walls. This is a very picturesque spot for a camp, or a break from hiking.

The trail continues to climb gradually until reaching about one mile below the lake. Here the trail crosses the creek again and then climbs steeply up the north wall of the canyon to Tin Cup Lake.

Tin Cup Lake is a large lake, about a mile long. It is located in a high steep walled basin. An irrigation dam and water control mechanism detract from the lake's appearance on the lower end.

There are several heavily used campsites just below the dam on the creek. The fishing is very good. There are also more campsites along the north shore next to the trail and at the upper end of the lake where a trail leads to a large clearing next to the creek above the lake. This site is also heavily used, especially by stock users.

Although the lake is very attractive and the fishing is good, my preference is to camp above the upper end of the lake a mile or two up the trail towards the pass. The trail begins a switchbacked climb shortly after it passes the upper end of the lake. As it climbs, it winds through a series of lovely open meadows. Among the meadows are some small streams and a few tiny pothole lakes. From some of the aspen fringed meadows, you can look back down at Tin Cup Lake. The area is rarely used for camping but offers excellent views and solitude.

To reach Triple Lakes on the Idaho side of the pass, simply continue on the switchbacked trail up the steep ridge west of the lake. The trail gains about 2,000 feet in about 2.5 miles from the lake. The Montana-Idaho border, at the top of the pass, runs along a high bare ridge. From here you can look to the west for a view of the upper end of the Triple Creek drainage and the Triple Lake below. From the ridge the trail gradually descends across an alpine meadow for about one-half mile, then begins a steeper drop across a bare west facing slope. The trail then leads directly to middle Triple Lake, a small high-mountain tarn which lies in an old glacial basin. This lovely high altitude setting offers several excellent campsites as well as good fishing. The other two Triple Lakes are relatively easy to find from here. Beyond the middle lake, the trail begins a very steep winding descent, dropping over 2,000 feet in about 2.5 miles. Close to the bottom of the descent, the creek enters a series of delightful cascades.

At the bottom of the descent is a flat, grassy area and a trail junction. There is an old trail that crosses Triple Creek here and leads south following White Cap Creek up to White Cap Lakes. There is an especially nice campsite here, very close to Patsy Ann Falls. The campsite is reserved for use by a commercial outfitter during the Idaho big game season and there are usually tents set up there by the first of September. If you get there earlier, it's a great place to camp. The trail leading to White Cap Lakes is very rough and poorly defined in places. It receives no regular maintenance. It follows White Cap Creek upstream for about three miles, climbing about 1,500 feet to the three White Cap Lakes. This is a very remote and isolated place in a lovely alpine setting. A good map and compass are necessary for this trek.

To reach the trail junction at Coopers Flat about twelve miles from here, follow the excellent trail downstream. This is a well maintained trail that follows along the north side of White Cap

Creek to the trail junction at Coopers Flat. The trail is a very easy hike, loosing only about 1,200 feet of altitude in about twelve miles. There are several nice campsites close to the creek, including one exceptional site next to the creek about six miles downstream from the Patsy Ann Falls area. This site is also occupied by the outfitter during hunting season.

Coopers Flat is located just above the junction of Canyon Creek and White Cap Creek. You will know you are there when you see the bridge crossing White Cap Creek. On the south side of the bridge is an old cabin. The cabin belonged to a trapper (you guessed it) named Cooper who trapped bears in this area. Cooper eventually traded his property with the Forest Service for a different location. The cabin is still in place and is scheduled for historical restoration. The cabin is secured with a locked steel jail-type door and rusty iron bars on the windows.

This is a good place to camp. There is a football field sized meadow in front of the cabin. It is a very pretty site for a camp. There is also a functioning outhouse located south of the cabin in the trees. This area is also used as a campsite by the outfitter.

A note of caution is in order here. This area has lots of bears. They visited my camp at night when I stayed here and I saw fresh footprints and several bears along the trails. The forest service trail crew also told me they had bear problems in this area.

From here you may follow Canyon Creek upstream to the Boulder Creek trailhead or go downstream along White Cap Creek to the trailhead at Paradise nine miles west of here.

To reach the Boulder Creek trailhead, about 21 miles east of here, take the Canyon Creek trail. The trail climbs steeply up to a bench just past the bridge over White Cap Creek. This is a fairly good trail but it is very lightly used. Because of the light use, the trail is somewhat overgrown and there were a number of logs across the trail when I hiked it in early September. Canyon Creek is a narrow canyon and the trail follows close to the creek. This is a good sized creek with deep pools and Volkswagen-sized boulders scattered throughout much of its length. Because the canyon is narrow, there are few good campsites available. The first one is about four miles east of Coopers Flat about 150 feet from the trail next to the creek. Another very good campsite is located about one-half mile further east, next to the creek and a small open meadow. There are a few more sites east of here as the canyon opens up a bit more.

About seven miles east of Coopers Flat, the trail begins to climb more steeply. More steep sections are encountered over the next several miles as you climb up to the pass leading to Boulder Creek. The top of the pass is about 7,400 feet in elevation.

About one-half mile east of the pass is a signed trail junction. The trail leading south is to Boulder Lake, about 1.5 miles from the junction. To reach Boulder Creek trailhead about nine miles from here, follow the good trail from the Boulder Lake trail junction to the east. It is all downhill from here! (See Boulder Creek for trail details.)

Topographic Maps. Darby; Burnt Ridge; Trapper Peak; Tin Cup Lake; Mount Paloma.

39. Chaffin Creek

This is a popular trail leading to three high lakes and some of the most spectacular scenery in the Bitterroots. The hike to the first lake is a very pleasant six mile trek. The round trip would make a nice day hike or would be an excellent overnight hike for a novice or casual backpacker. The trail is easy to follow and there are good campsites at the lakes. The scenery at the lakes is spectacular. Use is moderate.

Distances: See Map #6

Hart Lake *6*
Tamarack Lake *6½*
Chaffin Lake *7*

Trailhead Directions. From Darby, drive 4.4 miles south on Highway 93. Turn right on the West Fork Road. Go 100 yards, then turn right again onto a gravel road. This is the Tin Cup-Chaffin Road, although it is not identified here by a sign. Drive west 2.8 miles to a junction and take the right fork, where a sign indicates the "Tin Cup-Chaffin Road." The road is very good. Drive 1.1 miles to the trailhead sign for Chaffin Creek, located at a switchback. There are no facilities at the trailhead, and there is parking space for only a few vehicles along the road side.

Trail Description. The trail is well marked. It follows the north side of the creek. The grade is moderate for the first few miles, but the final climb to the lakes is steep. Most of the trail is in the trees, with occasional views of the canyon walls and the nearby peaks. However, after crossing a big rock field, you will begin to see spectacular snow covered peaks. The trail starts climbing more steeply and traverses several open rock faces. The path crosses the creek at the headwall at about five miles. Beyond the headwall, the trail climbs at a much more gradual rate. About one mile past the creek crossing the trail appears to end abruptly at a solid rock wall. A large waterfall is located on the north side of the rock wall. To find the trail again follow the base of the rock face to the south (the left side as you face upstream). This will lead to a steep, rough trail that skirts the south side of the rock face and reaches Hart Lake. The elevation gain from the trailhead to Hart Lake (elevation 7,336 feet) is about 2,600 feet. Hart Lake has a dam at the lower end and is marshy. It is not the best place to camp.

Tamarack Lake (elevation 7,425) is the largest of the Chaffin Creek trail lakes. It is almost one-half mile long and is reached by following the trail around the south side of Hart Lake and then walking upstream about one-half mile. Tamarack Lake is an exceptionally beautiful, high mountain lake with excellent campsites, beautiful views and good fishing. There is an old rock and mortar dam at its outlet. Cross the dam to access the north side of Tamarack Lake and to reach Chaffin Lake.

Chaffin Lake (elevation 7,505) lies about one-half mile upstream from Tamarack Lake. Chaffin Lake is a small, high alpine lake sitting at the upper end of the canyon. Steep rock walls and high, bare peaks to the west and north provide a lovely backdrop. Just follow the creek upstream to find Chaffin Lake.

Topographic Maps. Trapper Peak; Burnt Ridge.

40. Trapper Creek

This hike offers unique views of Trapper Peak and of a row of sharp tooth-like peaks on its north side. A relatively easy hike leads to a pleasant waterfall. Beyond that the trail is poorly maintained and very rough. Use is light.

Distances: See Map #6

First creek crossing..*2*
First and second falls....................................*2½*
Third falls..*2¾*
End of trail..*5½*

Trailhead Directions. From Darby, drive south on Highway 93 for 4.4 miles to the West Fork Road, Route 473. Turn right and drive 6.2 miles to the Trapper-Chaffin road (one half mile past the Job Corps Center). Turn right on this good gravel road. At .5 mile you will reach a "Y"-shaped junction. Keep left on the signed Trapper Creek Road. Drive 1.2 miles to the bridge. Cross the bridge and drive another 1.4 miles to the trailhead. The parking area has ample room and offers splendid views of Trapper Peak.

Trail Description. Trapper Peak remains immediately in front of you as you start up the trail. The first one-quarter mile offers continuous views of Trapper Peak on the south side and a row of jagged peaks and sheer rock cliffs lining the north rim of the canyon. Then the trees gradually close in on the trail offering only occasional views of Trapper Peak.

The trail climbs steadily at a moderate angle for the first two miles. The trail is a bit rough with rocks and roots underfoot. At about two miles the trail skirts the bottom edges of several rockslides offering splendid views of the peaks on both sides. Then it drops to the creek for the first stream crossing. There are logs available at this crossing, however the crossing angles upstream above the log crossing. It is easy to lose sight of the far side of the crossing here.

After the creek crossing, the trail is cluttered with fallen trees. Don't get discouraged. Another one-half mile of trail which climbs steeply in places, leads to a very pretty waterfall. The trail overlooks the falls. A small side trail leads to a second waterfall about 100 yards above the first falls. There is a pleasant shaded picnic spot overlooking these falls.

The trail follows a relatively flat easy section for one-quarter mile to another series of falls. Beyond the third falls, the trail crosses over to the south side and continues to climb steeply up into the canyon. This part of the trail is very rough with a great many down trees blocking the path. Rocks and roots make for a rough trail.

The trail continues to its end for a total of about 5.5 miles. It climbs steeply uphill right to its end. This trail does not appear to be regularly maintained.

Topographic Maps. Trapper Peak; Burnt Ridge.

41. Trapper Peak

The trail climbs steadily throughout its length, but at trail's end the rewards - sensational views from Trapper Peak - make this hike well worth the effort. The elevation gain from trailhead to peak is about 3,800 feet. Use is light to moderate.

Distance: See Map #6
Trapper Peak *5*

Trailhead Directions. The trailhead is twenty miles from Darby. Drive 4.4 miles south from Darby, on Highway 93 to Route 473, the West Fork Road. Turn right, drive 11.5 miles to Lavene Creek (Forest Road 5630), and turn right again. Follow this good gravel road for .6 mile to a junction. Take the left fork and follow the sign pointing to Troy Creek and Trapper Peak. Continue climbing on this road four miles to the trailhead, which lies just past a switchback and is marked by a sign. This trailhead is simply a wide spot with parking for a few cars. An excellent overlook point here provides a grand view of the Boulder Creek drainage.

Trail Description. The trail starts high on a ridge overlooking Boulder Creek (to the west) and the West Fork of the Bitterroot

River (to the south). It starts climbing steeply, following the ridge. For the most part it winds through trees but offers occasional views of the Boulder drainage and of Boulder Peak and other high, snowy crests. The trail is steep in places and is always a steady ascent. The size of the trees gradually diminishes with altitude, until at about three miles the trail emerges from a group of stunted, windswept alpine trees onto an open boulder field. For its last 2 miles the trail winds among the boulders above timberline and is well marked by rock piles. The final ascent to the peak follows an easily traversed ridge. To the north the view from the peak is of a sheer drop. Thousands of feet down lies a large, picturesque glacial cirque, surrounded by jagged, bare peaks. This spectacular view is well worth the climb.

Topographic Maps. Trapper Peak; Boulder Peak Piquet Peak.

42. Baker Lake

Although this is a rather short out-and-back hike, the course is not very heavily used because of its location and the difficulty of the trail. It provides access to some beautiful scenery in the Trapper Peak area and is a popular weekend spot for personnel from the nearby Job Corps Center. Fishing and camping at Baker Lake are good. If you are adventurous, you will enjoy following the creek to Middle Lake, then beyond to the creek's headwaters at tiny Gem Lake, which lies on a rocky shelf about one mile west of Baker Lake and about 500 feet higher. This is splendid alpine country. Use is moderate.

Distances: See Map #6

Trailhead Directions. From Darby, drive south on Highway 93 for 4.4 miles to the West Fork Road, Route 473. Turn right and drive seven miles west to the Baker Lake Road, which is signed . Turn right on the Baker Lake Road and drive about one mile to a junction. Take the right fork. Drive another mile to a second junction. Take the right fork again, and drive to the end, another 7.5 miles. This road gains a considerable amount of elevation, climbing the flank of the mountain via switchbacks. There is very limited parking and no trailhead facilities. There is no sign at the trailhead.

Trail Description. This trail is rough but well defined. It climbs steeply for the first quarter mile, then follows a more gradual slope for about one mile. The elevation gain in the 1.2 mile distance totals about 900 feet.

Although the trail is rough, it passes through attractive country. Some of the trail is in timber, but at several openings there are excellent views of Trapper Peak looming above to the west and of the Bitterroot Valley below.

Baker Lake is a high alpine lake at about 7,800 feet elevation. It is rather small, only about 200 yards long and about 100 yards across. It lies in a high glacial basin in an alpine setting, and sparse, dwarfed trees grow along its margin. Baker Lake is fed by a short chain of smaller lakes and ponds located upstream and to the west at the head of the canyon. Sheer massive rock walls loom above Baker Lake, while to the west high, jagged peaks and ridges form a monumental wall. The lake is reputed to offer very good fishing for cutthroat trout. There are several campsites at the lake.

To reach Middle Lake, follow Baker Lake's south (left) shore to the creek inlet. Much of the trail to Middle Lake is rough and poorly defined. Do not get discouraged. Just stay on the right side of the creek and follow it for .6 mile to Middle Lake, a lovely alpine tarn graced by the towering walls of Trapper Peak. This site offers good camping.

To reach Gem Lake, simply follow the creek feeding Middle Lake up a short steep canyon about .2 mile. Gem Lake, a true "gem" of the Rockies, lies at the base of Trapper Peak. It is nursed by perpetual snowfields even in late August. There is excellent camping and superb views.

Gem Lake probably is the loveliest of all the Bitterroot lakes. From here you can follow a stream to the flanks of Trapper Peak where, even in the heat of summer, "red snow" lies in long, steep fields.

Topographic Maps. Trapper Peak; Burnt Ridge.

43. Boulder Creek to Coopers Flat

Boulder Canyon offers some spectacular scenery and a good trail that follows close to the creek. About five miles up the trail is a very scenic spot next to a charming waterfall. The trail continues on to Boulder Lake which is a good camping area with beautiful scenic views. An exceptionally nice, 51 mile point-to-point hike is possible by hiking over the top of the pass into Idaho and connecting to the Tin Cup trail coming out at Tin Cup Creek trailhead near Darby. Use is moderate to Boulder Falls.

Distances: See Map #6

Trailhead Directions. From Darby, drive 4.4 miles south on Highway 93. Turn right on the West Fork Road (Route 473). Then drive fourteen miles southwest to the Boulder Creek Road, marked by a Forest Service sign for the Sam Billings Campground. Turn right and drive 1.4 miles north to the trailhead. There is a large parking area and a horse loading ramp.

Trail Description. The trail is well marked. It starts in a stand of huge ponderosa pines and follows the east side of Boulder Creek. For the first two miles the trail is very easy, climbing quite gradually. At about two miles the slope begins to increase and becomes moderately steep at about three miles. Here the trail emerges onto an open slope and offers views of the towering steep canyon walls. Boulder Peak looms to the west.

At about five miles, after a very steep uphill pull, you will emerge on a shelf next to a series of waterfalls. This is the lower portion of Boulder Creek Falls. This is a popular spot for campers and picnickers. There is an exceptional view of the waterfalls and the scenic walls of the canyon's west rim. A second waterfall is located about 300 yards above the first. There is a splendid deep pool below this waterfall with lots of small cutthroat trout. This is also a fine spot for sweaty hikers to take a cool, refreshing dip during the heat of a midsummer hike. The sheer rock walls on the west side of Boulder Canyon are decorated by slender, high waterfalls which spill from several tiny lakes located on inaccessible shelves high on the canyon wall.

The trail continues a gradual but steady climb for about three miles. The trail is easy to follow and runs mostly on the open, west-facing hillside, providing a view of Boulder Canyon and the surrounding peaks. At the upper end of Boulder Canyon the trail starts climbing steeply, high above Boulder Creek.

The trail junction to Boulder Lake is reached at about nine miles. The left fork, to the south, leads to Boulder Lake, about 1.5 miles from the junction. The Boulder Lake trail is marked by a Forest Service sign and leads downhill from the junction. The course passes a small pothole lake, then winds through an area that shows evidence of an old forest fire. Boulder Lake is easily located; it is a scenic high-mountain lake lying below a high peak and enclosed by high rock walls on the west and by sparse alpine trees on its lower end. Its beauty is somewhat marred by an old earth-and-rock irrigation dam eight feet high and by the ghostly dead trees of the old fire. There are good campsites at the lower end of the lake. There is moderately good fishing here, as well as lots of mosquitoes in late July.

To reach Coopers Flat eleven miles west of here and the White Cap Creek trail leading to Tin Cup Creek, continue west on the main Boulder Creek Trail. From the Boulder Lake junction the trail continues west up a steep course to the top of the pass. Here the trail provides spectacular views of Boulder Canyon to the east and of the surrounding peaks, including high, bare rocky ridges to the west.

The trail to Coopers Flat follows Canyon Creek for much of its length. From the top of the pass at the Idaho-Montana border, the trail descends a very steep slope. The trail has numerous switchbacks. About a mile east of the pass the trail crosses the upper end of Canyon Creek and then follows the creek closely to Coopers Flat. There are some good campsites along the five miles below the pass. There are few places to camp for the last five miles before reaching Coopers Flat.

Coopers Flat is located just above the junction of Canyon Creek and White Cap Creek. There is an old log cabin there and an open meadow. It is a good place to camp but there can be a bear problem here. There is also a bridge crossing White Cap Creek leading to the White Cap trail and the Tin Cup trailhead. For further details see Tin Cup to Boulder.

Topographic Maps. Boulder Peak; Mount Jerusalem; Tin Cup; Mount Paloma; Mount George.

44. Boulder Point

The hike along this high ridge to Boulder Point (7,750 feet) offers some spectacular vistas with a very good view of nearby Trapper Peak. The trail is very steep and gains a lot of elevation in a fairly short distance. The area is very lightly used so you should have it to yourself.

Distances: See Map #6
School House Point .... ¾
Boulder Point 2½

Trailhead Directions. From Darby, drive 4.4 miles south on Highway 93 to the West Fork Road, Route 473. Turn right, drive thirteen miles west to Barn Draw Road, and again turn right (north). Follow the signs for Boulder Point Lookout trail. The road ends at a locked gate.

Trail Description. The trail starts high on the north face of the slope overlooking the West Fork of the Bitterroot River. It climbs very steeply for the entire 2.5 miles, gaining about 2,500 feet in elevation. In about one-quarter mile, the trail reaches School House Point. From here you can view Boulder Creek Canyon below and the peaks to the northeast. The trail generally follows the ridge bordering the west side of Boulder Canyon, offering delightful views of this once-glaciated area.

Boulder Point is the site of an old lookout at about 7,750 feet elevation. From this vantage, there is a magnificent view of the surrounding area, including Trapper Peak.

Topographic Maps. Boulder Peak; Piquet Peak.

45. Nelson Lake

This is an excellent day hike over a relatively unused trail. It offers a sensational view of Nelson Canyon and the high Bitterroot peaks. The lake lies beyond a large prehistoric rock slide at the head of the canyon. The landscape of the lower slide features ghostly tree snags silhouetted against harsh grey boulders.

Distance: See Map #6
Nelson Lake...5 ½

Trailhead Directions. From Darby, drive 4.4 miles south on Highway 93. Turn right on Route 473, the West Fork Road, then go west fifteen miles and take the right fork at the "Magruder-Elk City, Idaho" sign. Proceed three miles and turn right at the "Gemmel Creek-Nelson Lake" sign. Go 2.7 miles and turn right.

Drive .3 mile to the Nelson Lake sign. Again turn right, and drive 2.4 miles to the Nelson Lake trailhead sign. This is a good road. Trailhead parking is limited, however, and there are no facilities.

Trail Description. At first the trail follows an old skid road, climbing steadily. Then it forks left and continues to climb through tree-shaded huckleberry patches. An invigorating (steep) two mile uphill walk leads to the ridge crest.

After taking in the lovely view of Nelson Canyon and the high peaks, you can follow the trail along the ridge for another half mile, then watch for tree blazes and cairns that indicate a trail junction. The right fork descends along the right side of the ridge to the canyon and Nelson Lake. (The left fork continues three miles along the ridge to a point directly above Nelson Lake. This is not the route to the lake.)

The trail into the canyon is not well maintained and is a little hard to find in places. The trail continues along an open hillside, affording a continuous vista of the surrounding area. Especially interesting is a prehistoric rock slide at the head of the canyon. You can reach the lake via a trail through the boulders along the west side of the slide. Nelson Lake is surrounded by heavy timber and by steep, rocky walls which ascend to the high peaks immediately above. Lake fishing for cutthroat trout is good.

Somehow the trail is harder to find going out than coming in, especially where it threads through the boulders. Watch for the cairns atop the boulders!

Topographic Map. Boulder Peak.

46. Watchtower Creek to Coopers Flat

Watchtower Creek trail is a charming place to hike. There is a good trail that follows the creek and climbs very moderately for the first 5.5 miles. The trail offers good views of dramatic steep canyon walls. There are several good places to fish and camp. Big horn sheep may be seen browsing on the canyon walls. A three mile side hike with no trail is available to Watchtower Lake by following the North Fork of Watchtower Creek. From the North Fork, the main Watchtower Creek trail climbs steeply to a pass into Idaho and then continues west to a trail junction leading to Coopers Flat about nineteen miles from the trailhead. This part of the hike is demanding, and involves a potentially dangerous creek crossing. From Coopers Flat, you may complete a long point-to-point hike to either the Tin Cup trailhead or Boulder Creek trailhead. Use is light.

Distances (from Watchtower Creek trailhead): See Map #6

Trappers Cabin at North Fork junction.........*5 ½*
Watchtower Lake *9*
Montana-Idaho Border *10*
Peach Creek Trail Junction *15*
Coopers Flat *19*
Boulder Trailhead..*39*
Tin Cup Trailhead..*49*
Paradise Trailhead *28*

Trailhead Directions. From Darby, drive 4.4 miles south on Highway 93 to the West Fork Road, Route 473. Turn right and drive southwest fifteen miles to the "Magruder-Elk City, Idaho" sign, about one-third mile past the West Fork ranger station. Take the right fork toward Elk City and drive west nine miles to the Watchtower Creek trailhead sign. Turn right and drive one-half mile to the trailhead, which has a very large parking area, a pit toilet, and a horse loading ramp.

Trail Description. This is a good, well-maintained trail that passes through very scenic country. It starts in widely spaced pines, mixed with aspens and follows Watchtower Creek to its headwaters. At one-half mile the trail crosses a good bridge to the stream's east side. The next two miles are through a forested area with little elevation gain. At about three miles, the trail emerges from the trees to pass avalanche chutes and talus slopes at the base of steep glaciated canyon walls. In places the trail is wet and muddy. The views of the canyon's walls are truly delightful along the next three miles. Watch for big horn sheep on the west side canyon walls.

At 5.5 miles, the trail changes direction swinging to the west and crosses three creeks in close succession. The third creek crossing is the largest. This is the North Fork of Watchtower Creek. For those interested in a side hike, there is a trail branching off to the north here, following the north fork to its headwaters at Watchtower Lake, located about three miles north of this trail junction

The North Fork trail follows the creek on its east side. The trail is poorly defined and not easy to follow. Watch for blazes on the trees and for cairns. The trail only lasts for about one mile and then it fades out. From the end of the trail to Watchtower Lake is another two miles north with no real trail. Consequently this hike is recommended only for experienced hikers who can use both maps and compass. Stay on the east side of the creek and follow a compass bearing of due north. The course runs through fairly heavy timber and up a very steep slope to a high shelf at the head of the canyon. There are short traces of an old trail every now and then. The last 200 yards involve crossing a sloped rocky face to a high alpine meadow about a mile long and one-half mile across. In an open meadow to the west lies Watchtower Lake, a small shallow body of water. Gently winding streams flowing from higher snowfields nurse this lovely isolated lake. To the north there is a rocky, steep mountain wall that marks the Montana-Idaho border. This is an exceptionally lovely area which is seldom visited. Elk and big horn sheep roam the area.

To continue hiking on the main Watchtower Creek trail, cross the North Fork to its west bank. Just past the creek crossing, a small log cabin nestles low in the trees to the left. This is an old trapper's cabin. It is only about four feet tall and to enter, you will need to crawl on your hands and knees.

Beyond the creek crossing and the cabin, the trail climbs steadily. The character of the plants changes as you enter the higher alpine zone. As you hike through this area, watch carefully for the big horn sheep that inhabit this area. About one-half mile below the ridgecrest is a grassy open area with streams and a small pond. This is a good place to camp.

The last half mile leading to the top of the pass is very steep. The total elevation gained from the trailhead ten miles back to the top of the pass is over 3,000 feet. However, the trail gains about 2,000 feet in the last four miles from the trapper's cabin crossing to the top of the pass.

From the top of the pass, which is the Montana-Idaho divide, the trail follows the ridgecrest high above the surrounding country. From here you can see Watchtower peak, which is very close, or dozens of other high peaks in the distance. Wherever you look there are continuous views of mountains that go to the horizon. The trail continues to the northwest for about one mile through splendid alpine terrain, with bare rock faces to the east and stunted windswept trees to the west. Some ghostly grey snags remain from an old fire.

After about 1.5 miles, the trail climbs briefly over Cooper Point and then starts to descend gradually through mostly open terrain. Here the trail is hard to find in places, especially where it passes through grassy sloping meadows. Watch for rock cairns and occasional blazes on trees. This is an excellent area for observing wildlife. The area is rarely visited by anyone except during hunting season.

About five miles from the Montana-Idaho border, the trail reaches a junction leading to Coopers Flat. This is the Peach Creek Trail. There is an old sign on a tree at the trail junction. Neither the sign nor the trail junction are easy to find, so watch carefully!

If you are interested in a long point-to-point hike, an option is to hike four miles down the Peach Creek trail to Coopers Flat. From Coopers Flat, you may continue up White Cap Creek and over the top of the Bitterroots to the Tin Cup trailhead. There are some potential obstacles to this hike that you should carefully consider. One possible problem is the creek crossing where the Peach Creek trail reaches Canyon Creek about one-third mile east of Coopers Flat. This can be a difficult crossing if the water level is up. By mid-August the water should be low enough for a safe crossing. Give it some thought!

Should you decide to take the Peach Creek trail north to Coopers Flat, head north and downhill from the trail junction. About one-quarter mile down the trail, past the junction, is a nice campsite with a good spring close by.

The trail down Peach Creek follows a ridge. It is a very steep trail that loses about 3,500 feet of elevation in about four miles. There is a burned area on this ridge and downfall may be a problem. The trail does not get regular maintenance so be prepared. As the trail descends it passes into heavily forested country.

At the bottom of Peach Creek the trail crosses Canyon Creek. The creek is about 25 feet wide here with lots of huge boulders. If you are very lucky you may find a log to cross on but don't count on it. The last time I forded here the water was almost waist high in places. When you reach the north bank of Canyon Creek, follow the dim path up the hillside until you reach the Canyon Creek trail. Turn left and follow this about one-third mile west to Coopers Flat. Here you will find a large open meadow with a log cabin and plenty of good places to camp. There is an outhouse south of the cabin and a bridge crosses White Cap Creek here. The cabin has a steel jail-type door over its front door and steel bars on the windows.

Although this is a nice place to camp, there are some potential problems for those who stay. The Coopers Flat area is reserved for use by a big game outfitter for the Idaho hunting season (September 15th). His tents are usually set up there by the first of September.

In addition, this area has lots of bears. The bears visited my camp at night the last time I camped there. A Forest Service trail crew told me they had bear problems in that area as well.

From Coopers Flat you have some trail options to consider. You may elect to head for the Tin Cup trailhead about 30 miles from here. To reach Tin Cup, cross the bridge over White Cap Creek and follow the White Cap Creek trail to the northwest over the crest of the Bitterroots to Tin Cup Lake and then down to the Tin Cup trailhead. For details of the Coopers Flat to Tin Cup hike see "Tin Cup Creek". A second option is to hike east along Canyon Creek trail and over the crest of the Bitterroots to the Boulder Creek trailhead 20 miles away. For details of the Coopers Flat to Boulder Creek trailhead hike, see "Boulder Creek Trail". A third option is to cross the bridge over White Cap Creek and hike downstream nine miles to the Paradise trailhead which is located to the west on the Selway River.

Topographic Maps. Mount Jerusalem; Watchtower Peak; Mount Paloma; Mount George; Burnt Strip Mountain.

47. Sheephead Creek to Indian Creek

This lightly used trail leads through forested country rich in wildlife. The route follows Sheephead Creek to its headwaters along the Idaho-Montana border gaining 1,900 feet of elevation. After reaching the State Line Trail a short descent leads to a charming campsite at the headwaters of Indian Creek. A base-camp at Indian Creek offers outstanding day hikes along the ridges above Indian Hill. Refer to Map # 6.

Distance: 7.5.

Trailhead Directions. From Darby drive 4 miles south on US-93. Turn onto the West Fork Road (473) and drive 15 miles west. Turn right at Nez Perce Road 0.3 mile past the West Fork Ranger Station. Drive 10.5 miles west and turn right at the sign, located just past the signed Fales Flat Campground. Drive up the access road for 300 yards to the unsigned trailhead at the end of the road. There is room for about 6 cars. A few rough campsites are available in an attractive setting near the creek. Stock facilities include a ramp and hitch rails. For those who wish to camp in the area you will find more facilities across the road in the Fales Flat Campground.

Trail Description. This trail follows an old jeep road for the first 400 yards. The trail then starts to climb a hillside with widely spaced trees. The route remains on the open hillside above the creek for almost 2 miles, before descending to a flat next to a creek crossing. This is the North Fork of Sheephead Creek. The crossing is about 25 feet wide and generally involves wading. I do not recommend wading this creek at high water, however at other times it is an easy crossing.

The trail climbs following the hillside well above the creek. It passes through a series of hillside meadows and scattered evergreen groves. Much of the route climbs and then dips. The trail along the hillside is well defined but the tread is quite narrow in places. At 3 miles the trail dips to cross a small creek. This area has several well-defined game trails that cross Sheephead Creek. Across the creek from the trail is a wooded bench 50 feet above the stream. The area contains mineral springs and mud wallows which seem to attract wildlife.

The trail continues much closer to the creek in more heavily forested country. At 4 miles there is a large extended campsite on a flat near the creek. At 5.5 miles the trail crosses the creek and ascends a lodgepole covered ridge. At 7 miles there is a signed junction with State Line Trail #16. Turn right and follow the State Line Trail downhill for 0.4 mile, through the trees to the campsite next to Indian Creek. The campsite is in a small clearing on the bank of the creek at the base of Indian Hill. A very steep trail leads up the open slope to the ridgecrest north of Indian Hill. This would make a very scenic day hike from your base-camp at Indian Creek.

Maps: USGS Watchtower Peak; and Nez Perce Peak.

48. Nez Perce Peak

This is one of my favorite ridgetop hikes, with outstanding panoramic views of the surrounding mountains. The route follows the Montana-Idaho border for 3 miles, passing through hillside beargrass meadows. A trail junction leads to the west along another ridgetop which is part of the Nez Perce Trail. After a final steep climb you arrive at the remains of the former lookout tower, providing an exceptionally fine 360 degree view point. This hike gains 1,800 feet in 6 miles. Refer to Map # 6.

Distance: 6.

Trailhead Directions. From Darby drive 4 miles south on US-93. Turn west on West Fork Road # 473 and drive 15 miles to the Nez Perce Road 468 located just west if the West Fork Ranger Station. Drive 16 miles to the top of Nez Perce Pass. There is a large paved parking area with room for over a dozen vehicles. There is a toilet available and stock facilities include a loading ramp and hitch rails.

Trail Description. Cross the road to the north side. The well-defined trail climbs steeply through a grove of widely spaced trees for 0.6 mile and then emerges in a large, open, hillside meadow. The route levels out a bit in the meadow. A very unobtrusive sign for Fales Flat trail junction is located at the northern end of the clearing. Stay left and continue hiking north. About 300 yards past the junction, on the left side of the trail, is an Indian grave with a marble headstone. This is the final resting place of Francis Adams, Salish Indian, who died at age 80 in 1900. The grave is outlined with small rocks. I have been told that there are other Indian graves nearby, however this is the only one with a marker.

The route climbs for another 0.2 miles beyond the gravesite and then follows more gentle rolling terrain. It continues through a series of open hillside meadows with grand views in every direction. When the beargrass plumes are in season the white flowers dominate the landscape. From this area Nez Perce Peak is clearly visible to the west.

The trail enters a wooded segment for 0.7 mile before reaching a signed trail junction. Turn left for Nez Perce Peak and follow the Nez Perce Trail west through the lodgepole forest. This trail follows a spur ridge leading all the way to the peak. The route winds through some trees and then crosses a large open hillside meadow and makes a steep descent through a grove of trees.

117

At 5.2 miles a steep climb leads to a saddle at the lower end of an open hillside. There is a campsite on the north side of the trail at the saddle. The view of the peak is blocked by the steep hill. A good spring is located about 400 yards southwest of the campsite on the south facing hillside. The trail from the campsite to the spring is quite dim and hard to find.

The route to Nez Perce Peak leads up the ridge past the campsite and then climbs through a hillside meadow where a 50 foot segment of the trail is not clearly defined. Just head uphill facing west and watch for the trail on the left. The remaining 0.7 mile segment is very easy to find as it climbs through an open grassy hillside.

At the top are the remains of an old lookout tower, including foundation stones, pieces of stove iron, broken glass, and chunks of wire. The peak offers an ideal spot to get oriented. Line up your map with a compass and see if you can locate the other lookout peaks, including Salmon Mountain, Spot Mountain, and Hell's Half Acre. If you look to the north you can easily see the broad grassy hillside of Indian Hill.

Map: USGS Nez Perce Peak.

49. Blue Joint Creek

This easy trail climbs gradually to reach lovely Blue Joint Meadows gaining only 1,100 feet of elevation in 10 miles. These mountain meadows are a great place to camp, fish and watch wildlife. The grassy clearings extend over a mile along meandering Blue Joint Creek. Clear water flows over a sandy bottom where deep pools provide good habitat for trout. Refer to Map # 11.

Distance: 10.

Trailhead Directions. Take US-93 to the junction with West Fork Road 473 located 4 miles south of Darby. Drive southwest 21 miles and follow the signs for Painted Rocks Lake. Turn right at the sign for Blue Joint Creek and drive across Painted Rocks Dam. Follow Road # 362 around the north side of the lake. At 2.5 miles take the second road to the left and follow Road # 362 signed for Blue Joint Creek. Drive 3 miles to the end of the road. The trailhead has room for 10 cars. A toilet and stock facilities are available. There is a trailhead sign for Jack The Ripper Creek.

Trail Description. The route starts on an old jeep road following the creek upstream. The trail skirts the base of talus slopes at the bottom of steep canyon walls staying very close to the creek and offers good fishing access. The steep canyon walls are mostly tree covered, with many tall granite cliffs towering above. The trail climbs very gradually except for a few short steep segments. At 3 miles the route climbs over some low cliffs, dips to cross a side creek, and then skirts the edges of some small meadows. Several nice campsites are located in this area.

At 4 miles just past the signed junction for Jack the Ripper Trail the trail crosses Jack The Ripper Creek. Continue upstream along Blue Joint Creek. The trail follows the creek closely, gaining elevation gradually. It is easy to follow as it ambles along the base of the hills. In a few places the trail climbs a bit to bypass cliffs next to the stream.

At 9 miles the trail cuts through a large meadow with a wide, shallow stream crossing. Wade across and climb the low forested rise. As the route descends on the other side of the rise watch for a well defined trail branching to the left. This leads through the trees and into Blue Joint Meadows which has several especially nice campsites. Blue Joint Creek runs clear over a sandy bottom, with deep pools at every bend in the meandering stream. This is a prime location for wildlife. I have often watched elk on the far side of the meadow in the early morning. Bears are also common.

If you miss the turn off, the main trail leads to a trailside camp at the upstream end of the meadow. From here you can see much of the downstream meadow enclosed by dense forest on 2 sides. The meadows are a charming place to camp. Fishing is good in Blue Joint Creek, however, the clear water in the deep pools requires a stealthy approach.

Maps: Frank Church, River Of No Return Wilderness; and Bitterroot National Forest

50. Piquett Lake and Slate Lake

This very steep trail leads to the ridgetop at the head of Little Boulder Creek climbing 2,850 feet in the process. From this elevated position it is an easy hike to both Piquette and Slate Lakes. These lovely high altitude lakes located at the base of Piquett Mountain offer scenic beauty and good fishing. Refer to Map # 12.

Distance: 5.5.

Trailhead Directions. Take US-93 to the junction with West Fork Road # 473 located 4 miles south of Darby. Drive southwest 21 miles and follow the signs for Painted Rocks Lake. Turn left at the sign for Little Boulder Creek just past Painted Rocks Dam. Drive one mile to the signed trailhead for Little Boulder Creek. Facilities include a stock ramp with hitch rails nearby and room for 7 vehicles.

Trail Description. The trail starts in a pleasant grove. At 0.3 mile it reaches a creek crossing. For the next half mile the trail climbs at a moderate rate, through a park- like area with widely spaced trees and with a great many huckleberry bushes. The canyon narrows considerably at the second creek crossing, spanned by a large log. For the next mile the trail climbs gradually along the hillside just above the creek and then it reaches a third dry footed creek crossing.

The trail follows a large switchback as it ascends a ridge leading away from the creek and then climbs steeply with little respite, all the way to the ridgetop. At 4.5 miles the trail reaches a saddle at the ridgecrest. A signed trail junction is located at the saddle. Turn right on Little Boulder Creek Trail # 55 and follow the ridgecrest uphill in a southeasterly direction. Three hundred yards past the first trail junction there is a signed junction with Piquett Creek Trail # 675. Stay on the ridge trail and continue up the steep ridge another 200 yards to reach an unsigned trail junction. Turn left and follow the steep trail down the rocky slope.

The route descends briefly and then climbs through a boulder field to cross a ridge. Descend the far side of the ridge to reach Piquett Lake. Some of the forested area near the lake was burned in the summer of 2,000. Piquett Lake, located just below Piquett Mountain, is small and round. I visited the area in late September and found a lovely mountainside of golden alpine larch shining in the sunlight above the lake.

To reach Slate Lake, follow the trail over the next ridge. At the low saddle on the ridge separating the two lakes is a nice campsite. It is only a few hundred yards from here down to Slate Lake. The lake is about 200 yards long and perhaps 100 yards wide. People I met there on my last visit assured me the fishing was very good.

Map: USGS Piquett Mountain

51. Crazy Creek to Twogood Cabin

This is an easy hike through a forested canyon with an attractive stream offering good fishing. This area is rich in wildlife. Moose are commonly seen along the creek bottom and beavers busily build new dams along the upper reaches of Warm Springs Creek. The trail leads to Twogood Cabin located in a picturesque meadow bordered by aspen trees. The trail gains only 400 feet in 6.2 miles. The cabin is available for rental from the Forest Service. To make a reservation call the Sula Ranger Station at (406) 821 3201. Refer to Map # 13.

Distances:
Sheep's Head Flat ....*2 ½*
Three Forks ....*5 ½*
Twogood Cabin *6.2*

Trailhead Directions. Drive on US-93 to 4 miles north of Sula and turn west on Medicine Springs Road # 5728. Drive 4 miles to Crazy Creek Campground. Follow the signs to trailhead parking. The parking area has room for 15 cars. There are stock facilities and a developed campground with drinking water.

Trail Description. Follow the road from the parking area to the toilet. The trailhead is next to the toilet where the pack bridge crosses Warm Springs Creek. The trail starts at the base of a talus slope and continues along a rock strewn path for 400 yards. The route then enters a forested area. This segment of trail offers good views the nearby creek.

At one mile there is a signed trail junction for Fire Creek. Stay to the right and cross the small creek on the convenient stepping stones. For the next 1.5 miles the trail remains smooth and wide, with little elevation gain. It is pleasantly shaded. Aspen trees grow among the jumble of rocks on the north facing slopes. This area was burned in the big fires of the year 2,000. The fires burned in a typical mosaic pattern, leaving the forest relatively intact.

At 2.5 miles the trail reaches Sheep's Head Flat, a very pleasant, large, grassy meadow, fringed by evergreens. This is a fine place for a picnic. At 3.5 miles you reach a creek. A flattened footlog with handrail allows a dry crossing. For the next 2 miles the trail follows the creek more closely as the canyon narrows, passing a series of beaver ponds along the creek bottom.

At 5.5 miles the trail reaches Three Forks Trail Junction. A footlog creek crossing leads to a clearing that has been used as a campsite. A trail junction sign is located in the clearing. Take the left fork for Porcupine Creek Trail # 205. From here it is 0.7 mile to the Twogood Cabin. Just follow the trail across the second footlog. This pleasant trail traverses a series of open meadows, passing even more beaver ponds along Porcupine Creek.

At 6.2 miles you reach Twogood Cabin, located in an attractive meadow near the creek. A small footbridge leads across the creek to the cabin. Stock hitch rails and an outhouse are across the creek from the cabin. The building is a partially restored line shack with a metal roof. It is small, with only 2 windows. It contains a stove and beds and has an outside bench in front.

Maps: USGS Medicine Hot Springs; and Bitterroot National Forest.

52. Porcupine Saddle to Crazy Creek

This is a point to point hike requiring a car shuttle. The hike starts near the top of the Bitterroots providing a downhill hike almost all the way losing 2500 feet of elevation in 11 miles. The trail leads over a ridgecrest and then descends a long series of switchbacks to reach Porcupine Creek. It passes through a very attractive series of grassy meadows bordered by aspen groves. Beaver dams are common along the creeks. The route leads to the Twogood Cabin, a partially restored line shack. The trail continues on to a pleasant clearing at Three Forks Trail Junction and then to the Crazy Creek Campground. The last 5.5 miles is an easy trail as it traverses a wooded canyon. Refer to Map # 13.

Distance: 11 miles one way.

Trailhead Directions. Crazy Creek Campground access. Take US-93 to 4 miles north of Sula. Turn west on Medicine Springs Road # 5728. Drive 4 miles to Crazy Creek Campground and follow the signs for trailhead parking. There is room for 15 cars. Stock facilities are available and the campground has drinking water and toilets. For the **Porcupine Saddle access** drive 4.5 miles south from Sula on US-93 to the Indian Trees Campground sign located 0.8 mile south of mile marker 8. Turn west and drive 0.7 mile to the campground. Turn left just before entering the campground and follow the sign for Porcupine Saddle. 0.6 mile past the campground take the right fork at the road junction. Follow Road # 8112 for 8 miles to Porcupine Saddle. It is a good road all the way. There is room for 12 cars. A stock ramp and hitch rails are available.

Trail Description. The trail starts in a burn blackened section of forest. The trailhead sign was gone when I last visited. The trail dips briefly to cross a creek and then climbs steeply to the ridgetop, reaching the saddle 0.5 mile from the trailhead. The ridgetop is a grassy hillside meadow. A trail sign is fastened to a tree at the saddle. The trail is poorly defined in this area. Head to the northwest, crossing the top of the ridge. The trail will soon become apparent along the western edge of the ridgetop meadows. Continue climbing uphill along the western edge of the escarpment. The trail is clearly defined and the views are especially good. At 1.5 miles there is a signed trail junction. Note that there are actually 2 signs here, one is designated "Three Forks Trail # 205" and the second is designated "Porcupine Creek Trail # 205". They are in fact the same trail. Turn left and follow Trail # 205 down the hill towards Porcupine Creek.

The trail follows an open ridge and then enters a forested area, where it descends more steeply. Numerous rubber water bars are installed along this next segment of trail. The descent continues through an extended series of switchbacks. This is a well-engineered trail with gentle switchback segments and a smooth tread, making for easy hiking.

At the end of the switchbacks there is a small creek crossing. The trail then follows Porcupine Creek down through a series of small meadows. The canyon gradually widens as the trail approaches Twogood Cabin at 4.7 miles. The structure is located in a broad meadow. An aspen grove is on one side of the clearing. An outhouse and stock facilities are across a narrow stream. A footbridge leads to the cabin. The small, metal roofed building is a partially restored line cabin. The cabin is available for rental from the Forest Service.

A pleasant and easy three quarter mile jaunt leads downstream through more meadows to a good footlog bridge at Three Forks Trail Junction. After crossing the first creek the trail continues through an attractive clearing where a trail junction sign is attached to a tree. This is the junction for Warm Springs Trail # 103. Take the right fork for Crazy Creek Campground. (The left fork leads up and across a divide to Overwich Falls). Cross the second footlog and follow the good trail downstream. A series of dams along the creek bottom indicate an active colony of beavers. At 7.5 miles there is a creek crossing with a good footlog bridge.

The remaining segment of trail is fairly smooth and flat. At 8.5 miles the trail reaches Sheep's Head Flat, a wide pleasant meadow. A trail sign is fastened to a tree. At 10 miles you reach the Fire Creek Trail junction just past a small creek crossing. At 11 miles there is a good stock bridge crossing Warm Springs Creek to Crazy Creek Campground.

Maps: Bitterroot National Forest; USGS Medicine Hot Springs; and Sula

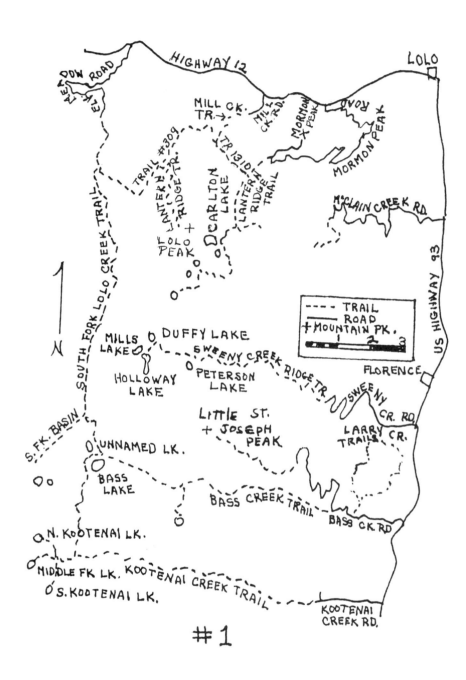

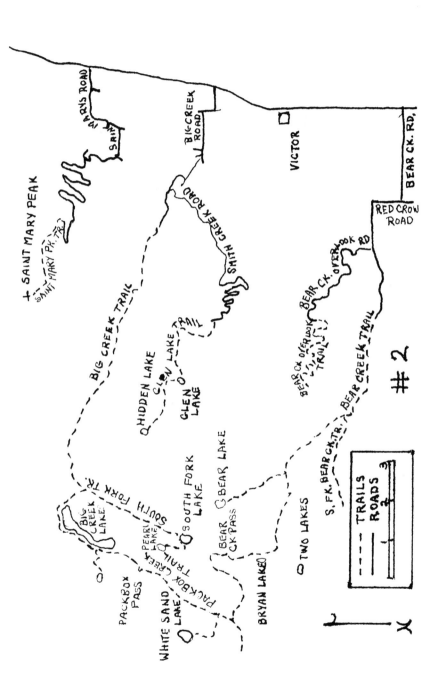

SAINT MARY PEAK

SAINT MARY PK. TR.

MARYS ROAD

SAINT

BIG CREEK ROAD

SMITH CREEK ROAD

BIG CREEK TRAIL

HIDDEN LAKE

GLEN LAKE TRAIL

GLEN LAKE

VICTOR

BEAR CK. RD.

RED CROW ROAD

BEAR CK. OVERLOOK RD.

BEAR CK. OVERLOOK TRAIL

S. FK. BEAR CK.TR.

BEAR CREEK TRAIL

SOUTH FORK TR.

BIG CREEK LAKE

PEARL LAKE

SOUTH FORK LAKE

BEAR LAKE

BEAR CK PASS

TWO LAKES

PACKBOX CREEK TRAIL

PACKBOX PASS

WHITE SAND LAKE

BRYAN LAKE

TRAILS
ROADS

1 2 3

#2

N

128

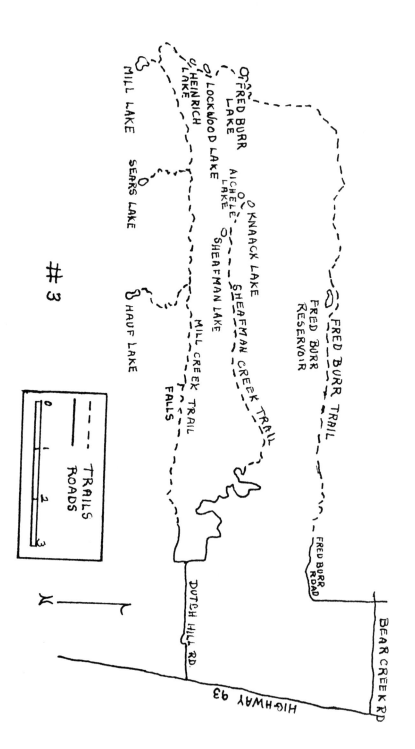

3

MILL LAKE

HEINRICH LAKE

FRED BURR LAKE

LOCKWOOD LAKE

SEARS LAKE

AICHELE LAKE

KNAACK LAKE

SHEAFMAN LAKE

HAUF LAKE

SHEAFMAN CREEK TRAIL

FRED BURR RESERVOIR

FRED BURR TRAIL

MILL CREEK TRAIL FALLS

FRED BURR ROAD

DUTCH HILL RD.

BEAR CREEK RD

HIGHWAY 93

N

0 1 2 3

TRAILS
ROADS

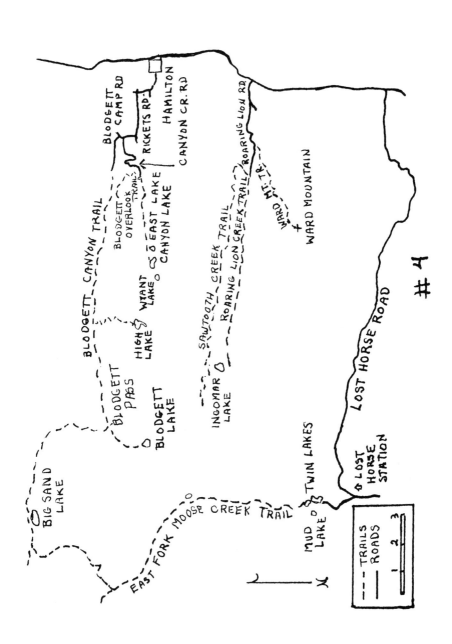

BLODGETT CAMP RD
BLODGETT CANYON TRAIL
RICKETS RD.
HAMILTON CANYON CR. RD
BLODGETT OVERLOOK TRAIL
EAST LAKE
CANYON LAKE
WYANT LAKE
HIGH LAKE
BLODGETT PASS
BLODGETT LAKE
SAWTOOTH CREEK TRAIL
ROARING LION TRAIL
ROARING LION CREEK TRAIL
ROARING LION RD.
WARD MT. TR.
WARD MOUNTAIN
INGOMAR LAKE
BIG SAND LAKE
EAST FORK MOOSE CREEK TRAIL
MUD LAKE
TWIN LAKES
LOST HORSE STATION
LOST HORSE ROAD

#4

TRAILS
ROADS
1 2 3

130

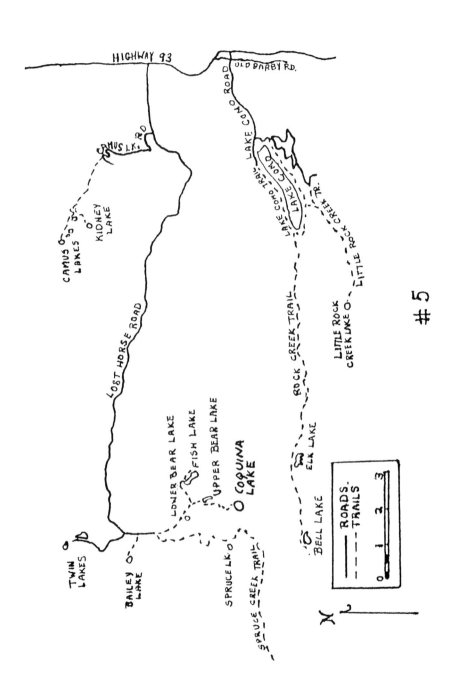

HIGHWAY 93

OLD DARBY RD.

LAKE COMO ROAD

CAMUS LK. RD.

CAMUS LAKES

KIDNEY LAKE

LOST HORSE ROAD

LAKE COMO TRAIL

LAKE COMO

LAKE COMO TRAIL

LITTLE ROCK CREEK TR.

LITTLE ROCK CREEK LAKE

ROCK CREEK TRAIL

LOWER BEAR LAKE

FISH LAKE

UPPER BEAR LAKE

COQUINA LAKE

ELK LAKE

BELL LAKE

SPRUCE LK.

SPRUCE CREEK TRAIL

TWIN LAKES

BAILEY LAKE

ROADS.
TRAILS

0 1 2 3

N

5

131

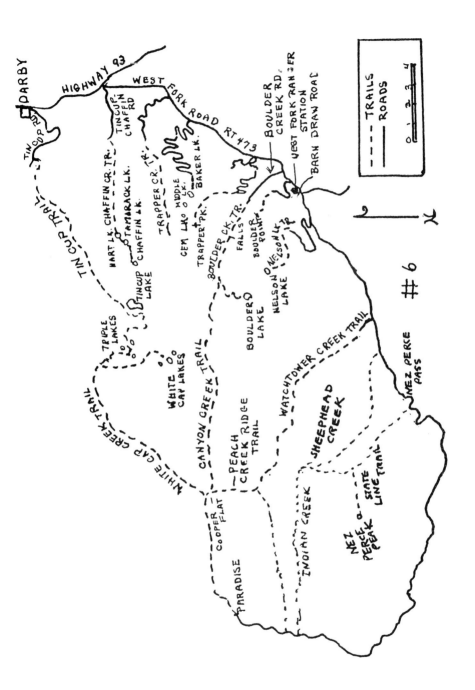

DARBY

HIGHWAY 93

WEST FORK ROAD RT 473

TIN CUP RD.

TIN CUP TRAIL

TINCUP CHAFFIN RD

HART LK. CHAFFIN CR. TR.

TAMARACK LK.

CHAFFIN LK.

TINCUP LAKE

TRAPPER CR. TR.

CEM LK.O MIDDLE O LK.

BAKER LK.

TRAPPER PK.

BOULDER RD.

WEST FORK RANGER STATION

BOULDER CREEK RD.

BARN DRAW ROAD

BOULDER CK. TR.

FALLS

BOULDER POINT

NELSON O NELSON LAKE LK.

TRIPLE LAKES

WHITE CAP LAKES

BOULDER LAKE

CANYON CREEK TRAIL

WHITE CAP CREEK TRAIL

PEACH CREEK RIDGE TRAIL

WATCHTOWER CREEK TRAIL

SHEEPHEAD CREEK

NEZ PERCE PASS

COPPER FLAT

INDIAN CREEK

NEZ PERCE PEAK

STATE LINE TRAIL

PARADISE

TRAILS
ROADS

0 1 2 3 4

N

6

132

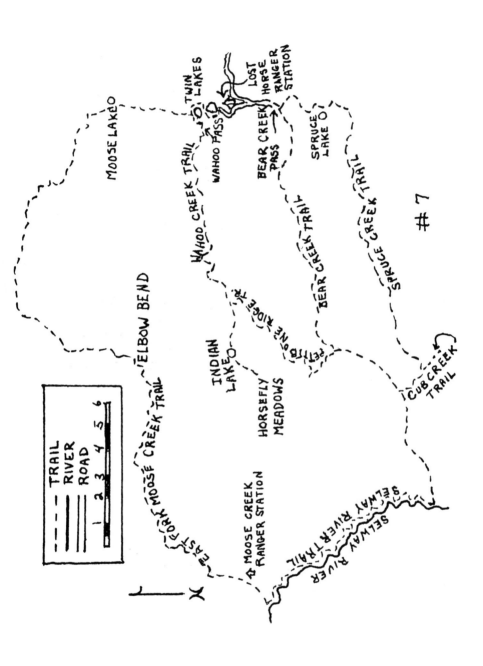

MOOSE LAKE

TWIN LAKES

LOST HORSE RANGER STATION

WAHOO CREEK TRAIL

WAHOO PASS

BEAR CREEK PASS

SPRUCE LAKE

SPRUCE CREEK TRAIL

#7

ELBOW BEND

BEAR CREEK TRAIL

BONE RIDGE

INDIAN LAKE

CUB CREEK TRAIL

HORSEFLY MEADOWS

EAST FORK MOOSE CREEK TRAIL

MOOSE CREEK RANGER STATION

SELWAY RIVER TRAIL

SELWAY RIVER

TRAIL
RIVER
ROAD

1 2 3 4 5 6

133

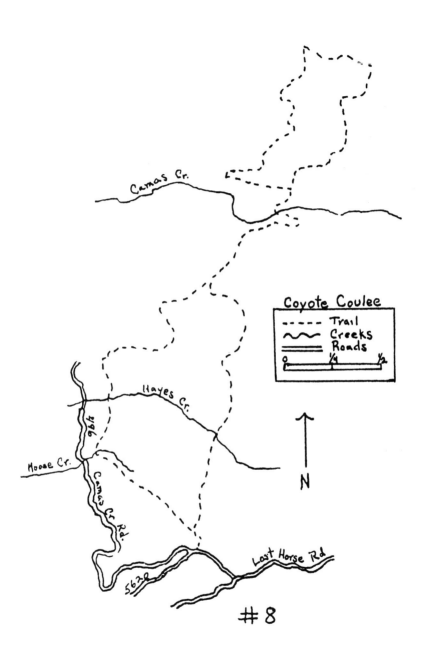

Camas Cr.

Coyote Coulee

- - - - Trail
~~~~ Creeks
===== Roads

0   ¼   ½

Hayes Cr.

964

Moose Cr.

Camas Cr. Rd.

N

Last Horse Rd

5628

#8

134

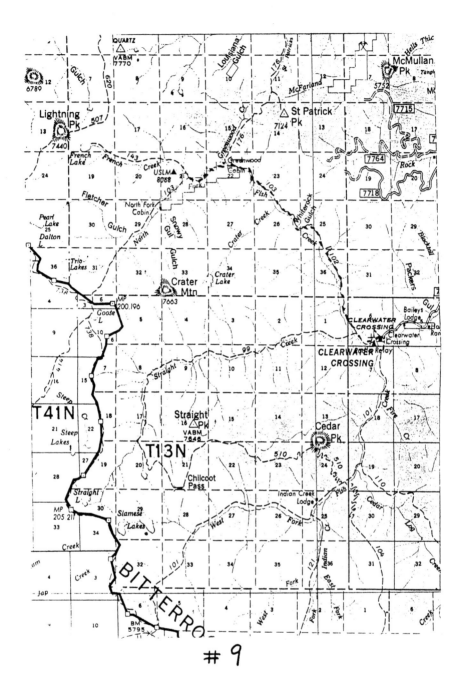

9

135

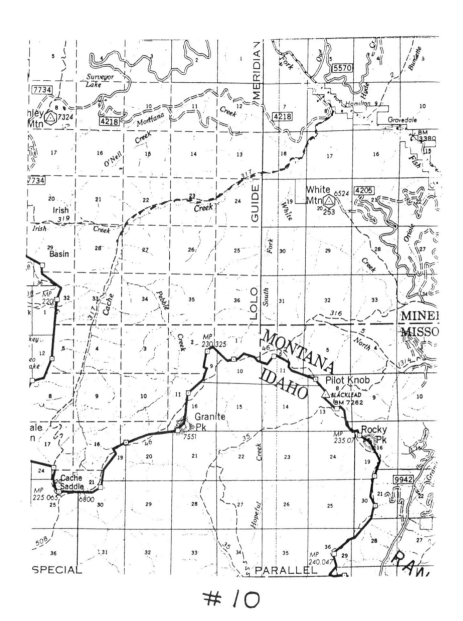

10

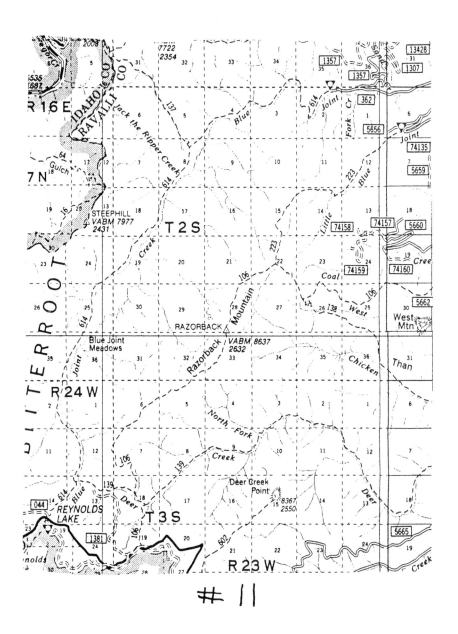

11

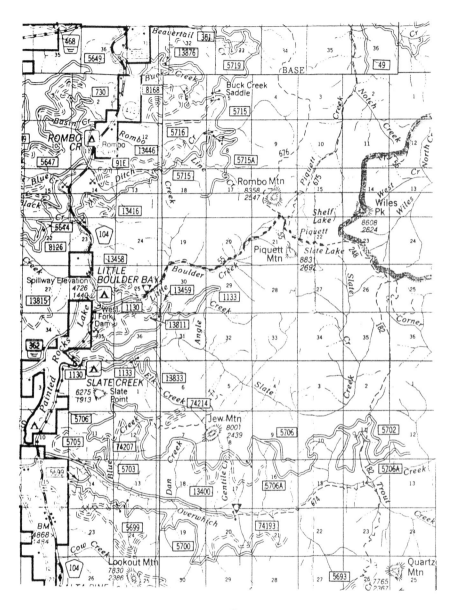

12

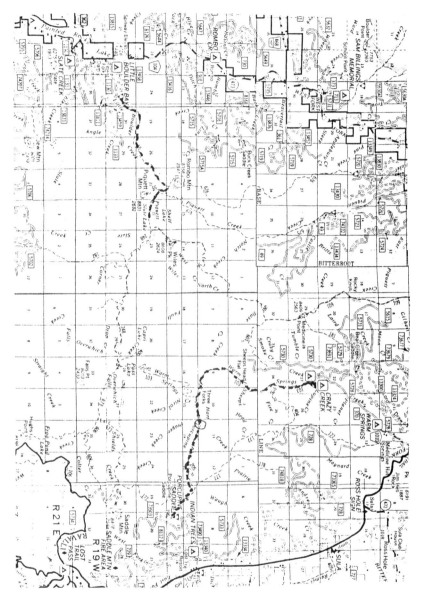

#13

139